Taking Intentional Action

How to Choose the Life You Lead

Desiree Petrich

Aurora Corialis Publishing

Pittsburgh, PA

TAKING INTENTIONAL ACTION: HOW TO CHOOSE THE LIFE YOU LEAD

Printed in the United States of America

Edited by: Allison Hrip, Aurora Corialis Publishing

Cover Design: Karen Captline, BetterBe Creative

Paperback ISBN: 978-1-958481-29-5

Ebook ISBN: 978-1-958481-30-1

ADVANCE PRAISE

"Desiree's book is an amazing reflection of her own life experiences and how she took control of her life and found happiness. She shares personal stories about her weight loss journey, the relationship she had with her mom, and several others that are interesting and informative. Desiree gives examples and advice to help you see that you must figure out where you are in your life, examine what your goals are, and eliminate excuses that are holding you back. She shared, 'Happiness is not mutually exclusive with anything.'

"From physical health to personal development, Desiree's book encourages you to make your life your own. You own your purpose, and you develop your journey. This is a must read on life and how to improve yourself, because the only person who can really do that is you. You are truly in control of your own life."

–Holly Hoffman, Professional Speaker and Author

———

"I DARE you to read *Taking Intentional Action* and try to *not* find yourself within this book. From the moment you crack open its pages, prepare to embark on a journey of self-reality like no other. With every chapter, you'll find yourself nodding in recognition, struck by the uncanny feeling that this book was penned specifically for you. Whether it's confronting your excuses, seeking your purpose, or navigating the pitfalls of leadership, *Taking Intentional Action* holds a mirror to your inner thoughts and challenges you to confront them head-on. This book empowers you to shed the masks you wear and embrace your authentic self. But this is more than a dare—it's a challenge to elevate your influence and impact."

–John Beranek | Founder, Intersections Consulting

———

"*Taking Intentional Action* is a captivating guide that empowers readers to take control of their lives and create the future they desire by being intentional and building a life you love from the bottom up. Through insightful reflections and actionable steps, Desiree illuminates the importance of intentional living and provides practical strategies for setting meaningful goals, cultivating positive habits, and overcoming obstacles. With a blend of personal anecdotes and motivational wisdom, Desiree inspires readers to embrace purposeful decision-making and design a life filled with fulfillment and joy. Whether you're seeking direction in your career, relationships, or personal development, Desiree offers invaluable guidance for anyone ready to embark on a journey of self-discovery and transformation.

—Melissa Maranell, LSW I Hospice Agency Manager

———

"If you are looking to connect on a deeper level to your soul's purpose, this book is for you! The raw, vulnerable, and yet, positive message Desiree shares will be impactful for anyone who has gone through hard things, to remind them that there is always a silver lining, but we have to intentionally look for it. There is always a way we can do and be better."

—Jessica Burgio | Holistic Life and Business Coach

———

"Our personal development is a lifelong journey. No matter where you are on your journey, *Taking Intentional Action* is a resource you must revisit often. (Get your highlighter and post-its ready!)

"While we have good intentions to live a happy life, our daily chaos, self-sabotage, and unexpected challenges will undoubtedly throw us off course and into overwhelm.

"Desiree reminds us that we are ALWAYS able to choose how we show up to our life. Her highly practical self-leadership framework and guidance will both motivate and challenge you to get real with who you are, ditch the excuses, own your inner leader, and take intentional action each day to build a life you love. No matter what curveballs life throws your way—you absolutely can build the emotional resilience and wherewithal to live a happy life—at home and work!"

–Merilee Smith, Leadership & Mindset Coach | Speaker | CEO Coach with Merilee

———

"If you are looking for a book that's got heart + depth, but at the same time gives you the tools and mindset shifts to work through the hard times in life, THIS IS IT."

–Katy Fassett | Health and Wellness Coach

DEDICATION

I would like to dedicate this book to the following people:

My mom

She was my best friend, the grandma to my babies, my role model, and the person I called multiple times a day for no reason at all. She was the embodiment of everything I want to be. Kind, generous, smart, driven, and selfless. I will continue to miss her every day, but for the things she taught me and the love she gave, I will forever be thankful to her.

Mom, I miss you.

My husband

James is my rock, my best friend, my biggest supporter, and the reason I have been able to live out my dream. Our kids are so lucky to have him as their dad, and I am the luckiest girl in the world to be able to call him mine.

James, thank you for helping me build this life that we love.

My kids

Brenna and Owen are my reason for everything. They are my daily reminder to slow down and be thankful. They are my light in moments of darkness, and my reason for laughter and adventure. I will forever be thankful for them and the meaning they have brought to my life.

Brenna and Owen, thank you for making me a mom.

TABLE OF CONTENTS

INTRODUCTION - MY STORY

If you would have asked me on February 21, 2022, *What's the hardest thing you've ever had to do?* I would have told you that it was managing a dementia facility through COVID-19.

But then, on February 22, 2022, my son was born during a Minnesota blizzard. His birth could have been the end of a happy story, but five minutes after he was born, we were told his left lung hadn't expanded during the delivery, and he needed to go to the neonatal intensive care unit (NICU). Unfortunately, the hospital he was born in did not have a NICU or the equipment to help him. We had to transfer to another hospital, 90 minutes away.

From the nearly 20 hours our baby boy fought for his life before getting the help he needed in the other hospital's NICU, to four weeks later when my mom had her first stroke (just 24 hours after we returned home with our healthy son), my life was never the same. It's amazing how one day—one moment—can set off a string of events that will change your life forever.

Regardless of when you read this book, if you were to ask me *now* about the hardest thing I've ever had to do, I would tell you it is living in a world without my mom. My family suffered many losses soon after. We went to six funerals in the following two years, for reasons including suicide, heart attacks, ALS, diabetes, and organ failure. I could easily let this pain be my story. But I have learned from these experiences that the same circumstances (often outside of our control), that have the potential to break us into a million pieces, also hold the secrets to our growth and self-awareness. Inside these difficulties lie the tools we need to overcome adversity, remain humble and grateful, be intentional in every moment, and learn to lead. We lead in many ways: with our children, and our teams, and more importantly, ourselves.

I didn't know it at the time, but I had been preparing for these events. For three years prior to my son's birth I had been reading personal development books, falling in love with health and fitness, finding the courage to embark on journeys that terrified me, and learning lessons through the successes and failures I experienced along the way.

I hadn't always viewed life in such a positive and optimistic way. I have spent a lot of time and effort over the years trying to become a better version of myself. I had gained and lost 50 pounds at least four times in my life. For years after graduating, I thought college was a big waste of time and money. I spent the majority of my life trying to be friends with everyone because I was too afraid to risk someone not liking me for me.

There was a catalyst to the changes I have made in order to say that I love the life I am living, but they weren't made in the course of a day. They were made over a period of years of intentionality. The changes were made in succession: one mistake and lesson made after the other before they started to compound into what not only looked like success on the outside but felt like happiness on the inside.

Without this work, the events of the following years could have easily broken me. I don't think anyone would have blamed me for falling into depression, pulling away from relationships I had cultivated, letting dust pile up on the books on my desk, and no longer exercising. To be honest, I'm surprised that I didn't.

Somehow, through all the pain, I had retained my ability to be grateful and thankful. I continued to feel moments of joy and to laugh out loud. I wrote songs as *love letters* to my mom that I now sing to my kids every day. I became more intentional about reaching out to the people I love when I thought of them, making sure they know they're loved.

I didn't just want that ability for myself, though, I wanted to help others build a life they love without feeling like they had to start over every time something bad happened or like they were constantly picking up the pieces, especially not by themselves. So, I reverse-engineered my experience. I began to write down my process for building a life I love from the ground up. I included my weight-loss journey, starting at 275 pounds in junior high to becoming a fitness instructor and someone who lists exercise as her hobby. I included my journey from an inexperienced and unqualified manager to managing a healthcare facility through the pandemic. I included my story of becoming a mom after being told I would likely never have kids because of a *common* hormonal condition I didn't know I had until after an emergency surgery almost took my life. I laid out everything—from beginning to end, good to bad, and everything in between. I drew out what it would look like if I had to start all over again, and the Foundation of Self Framework was the result. The framework shows how to build a strong foundation for your life in three tiers, including *self-engagement*, *self-worth* and *self-awareness*.

I use this framework routinely in my leadership development business. Companies are starting to realize that the health of the organization is directly correlated to the health and happiness of their employees. Incorporating the Foundation of Self Framework has allowed me to help both emerging and experienced leaders create confidence at home, as well as work.

Tier one is self-engagement. It is the foundation that everything else it built on. These are the habits and mindset shifts we intentionally put in our lives to start closing the gap between where we are and where we want to be. We must engage with the process of building healthy habits in all areas of our lives.

Tier two is realizing your self-worth. This tier establishes a practice of redefining success in a way that is attainable, realistic, and exciting! It's a practice of understanding that your self-worth is not tied to any external validation. Self-worth is not about *learning* to love yourself or *working* hard enough to deserve self-love, but recognizing you are uniquely and unequivocally yours, and that is the most precious type of love. It is unconditional, or at least it should be. We will work on strengthening that love in the second tier of the Foundation of Self.

Love is a verb, not only in the context of loving yourself, but from the workplace and back again to our homes and children. Yes, love is a feeling, but it's also a set of actions we instill in our lives, regardless of how we feel in the moment. Defining success in a way that makes us excited to continue the process of loving ourselves to the best of our ability is what makes tier two both tangible and sometimes intangible.

Tier three is about developing self-awareness, which includes learning to trust yourself, and emotional and social intelligence. Let's talk about trust. It is imperative you learn to trust yourself. Ask yourself, *Is my trust unconditional?* Do you trust yourself completely? Do you trust others? Build a foundation strong enough that you are confident in your ability to trust yourself and others.

How is your emotional intelligence? Emotional intelligence is your ability to understand emotions, both your own and those around you. I view it as an ability to have a conversation with yourself and coach yourself through a problem. Ask yourself if you don't like the thoughts going through your head, are you able to redirect them to a thought of your choosing? When faced with a task that you don't want to do, can you access your original motivation (the concept, not the feeling)? Do you know how to ask yourself questions that can help you work through anxiety, frustration, and feelings of imposter syndrome? Having a high emotional intelligence means you look at how you can develop your strengths to reach your goals and help those around you do the same. It's also being able to look at your weaknesses not as a hindrance to your success but an opportunity to learn more about yourself and your limitations.

How is your social intelligence? Social intelligence is when you enter a social situation, and you can see more than just your own placement in the room. How can you meet people where they are? How can you add to the conversation without overstepping boundaries? How can you be a good mix of a listening ear and a voice with something to say? Many of us struggle with how to do this. Are you like me, putting your foot in your mouth more often than you'd like to admit? Are you able to apologize after you do? Can you read a room and determine the energy? Can you lead with confidence, even in potentially uncomfortable situations? Social intelligence is about making decisions in social situations that elevate all the people in a room, including you.

You'll likely never reach a point where you can say with absolute certainty, *I trust myself 100 percent, I am emotionally intelligent,* or *I am socially intelligent.* The process is never ending. You will practice these things for the rest of your life. That should excite you! This is your opportunity to revisit the way you think about failure, embarrassment, guilt, jealousy, etc. There are always new tools you can add to your toolbox to continue growing in your trust and intelligence.

Growing into emotionally and socially intelligent people who love and trust themselves unconditionally is an important aspect of building a solid foundation! But what about happiness? What role does happiness play in our lives and our foundation of self? Is it, or should it be, the ultimate goal? Often, we place our entire life's worth on our ability to be happy. We put an incredible amount of pressure on our ability to raise happy children, and, yet, we place contingencies on our happiness, saying things like *I'll be happy when*, or *I would be happy if*.

Happiness is not a destination we are trying to reach. It is a state of mind. Placing happiness as the ultimate goal makes it appear too far out of reach, maybe even to the point we feel it's not worth striving for. We get the choice to reframe what it means to be happy by letting go of the idea that it's something we have to earn. We come to understand it is tied to our intentions, and our intentional actions, as opposed to the results that we often don't have control over. When we do this, we begin to understand what it means to build a life where happiness is always attainable, but never guaranteed. It's up to us.

My favorite part of the whole process has been the continuation of it. Through every lesson I learn, every relationship I cultivate, every mistake I make, every tear I shed, and every book I read, I get to continue learning, growing, and strengthening my *Foundation of Self* ... and so can you.

I realize now that the events that occurred will always be a part of my story, as will the events that follow. As humans, there is only one thing we can be certain of ... and that's uncertainty. The only guarantee that we have, is that life will throw us curveballs. But there is one thing we have that life, humanity, and adversity cannot take from us: our ability to control our own happiness and build a life that we love, regardless of the circumstances outside of our control.

You will notice that I use the plural pronouns, such as *we* and *our* during the majority of this book. I have done this for a few reasons. One, every single example I have given is one that I have experienced. They are thoughts, actions, and conversations that I have had with my family, friends, and others I have interacted with over the years. Reason number two, is to ensure that *you* know that you are not alone. Personal leadership, along with choice, and intentionality, are the overarching messages of this book. While those things are specific to us as individuals, we need to know that even while we lead ourselves to our decisions and choices, we don't ultimately have to do it alone.

Whether you are a parent, friend, student, teacher, coworker, or leader, if you are looking to elevate your influence in your home and your work, this book is for you, and those are just the extra benefits. I can't wait to join your journey of intentional action toward self-engagement, discovering your self-worth, and building your self-awareness.

CHAPTER 1: EVALUATE YOUR EXCUSES

"When it comes to barriers to success, we are usually our own
worst enemies."1
- John Maxwell

When you look at your life, are you happy with where you are
and what you've accomplished? If not, what do you attribute your
lack of success to? Hearing that you are the barrier to your own
success can feel offensive. It's like someone telling you that *you're
the problem*, and then walking away without saying, *just kidding*. If
you don't feel as though you are living up to your full potential and
living out your purpose, it can be triggering to hear someone say
that it's your fault. It's much simpler to blame it on life, and the
circumstances that have been out of your control up until this
point. It's one thing to feel inadequate when you contemplate your
life and the things you've accomplished; it's another to have
someone point out that you are likely the problem. It hits hard
because we know it's true. At least it was for me.

When I was 275 pounds in eighth grade, I would have told you
that it was due to circumstances outside of my control. My parents
bought me too much candy and junk food at the gas station. There
weren't enough opportunities to exercise. I was moving schools for
the third time in three years, and the stress was getting to me. But
what I wasn't saying out loud was that I did not want to be out of

---

1 John Maxwell, *The 15 Invaluable Laws of Growth: Live Them and
Reach Your Potential* (New York: Hatchett Book Group, 2012), 30.

shape and overweight. I would have loved to fit in with the girls and be looked at by the boys. I would have loved to be considered a good volleyball player and had something to look forward to other than watching TV when I got home at night. Up until this point, I don't recall ever trying to lose weight. I don't remember ever having been told that I had a problem. How do you tell a 14 year old they're fat?

What I do remember is trying out for volleyball in eighth grade and being told that in order to play, I would have to be able to quickly get up off the ground after diving for a ball. I had to be confident enough to stay on my feet when the ball came near me, plant my feet, and choose the direction I wanted the ball to go. I was told I had to use both arms to play, and not just swing an arm out every time the ball came in my direction. (Hindsight—these are great metaphors for life that were completely lost on an eighth grader!)

I remember one specific day of practice when the coaches told us that we should try to avoid pop and candy for one week, just to see how it affected us. They explained why it might have a negative effect on us at first, but if we pushed through, it would increase our energy levels.

I have not had a pop since 2006 ... and I lived for my nightly pop. So how could a 14-year-old girl, so overweight she had a hard time getting up off the ground, quit cold turkey? (And yes, I realize how Minnesotan it is to say *pop* instead of *soda*!) The answer: someone explained why I should.

I dropped 18 pounds within one month from this change alone. It's not about doing something because someone says we should, or not doing something because someone says we shouldn't. Understanding ourselves, our limitations, and our motivations is key to tapping into what's right for us as an individual. It's about listening to information and analyzing our options. Following someone's advice (or not following their advice) is a *choice* we get to make.

When I started to feel better and moving became a bit easier, it occurred to me that being overweight was also a choice. Feeling like the victim was a choice. Not doing anything about it was a choice. Making excuses for why I wasn't able to change was a choice. After being able to move easier, you might expect to learn I made the team, but it didn't quite work out that way. I've heard it said that *Progress is made daily, not in a day.* It was going to take more than one volleyball season to see the kind of change I was striving for in my life, but the important part was that I was choosing to change.

I spent the majority of that next summer alone, refusing to allow the old excuses to dictate my future. I had seen the alternative, and I wasn't willing to turn back. I spent the summer running (I started by barely being able to run to the mailbox less than a block away). By the end of the summer, I had lost a lot of weight and developed habits that I still practice today. That summer was the beginning of a physical, mental, and emotional journey that took me way outside my comfort zone.

I know better than anyone that moving within your comfort zone feels safe. It is a lateral move because if you don't change what you're doing, then nothing will change! How many times have you told yourself that you'll start on Monday? Or set a new year's resolution that things will be different this year? How many times have you found an accountability partner (because that's what all of the books tell you to do), only to feel guilty when you don't follow through on your end? How many times have you lost weight, only to gain it all back, plus some? How many times have you started to read a book, only to be upset when it's still on your nightstand a month later with the bookmark on the second page?

I'm guessing at this point you feel like I'm bullying you. I know because all of those examples are personal to me. Through years of trying and failing, some of the hardest lessons I've learned still surface, usually right after I feel like I've finally gotten things all figured out. Here's the thing, life won't wait for us to *feel* caught up. We have to choose to take responsibility for the things in our lives, even when we don't feel like it. No one knows us better than we know ourselves. We have to find a way to hold ourselves (and others) accountable to the decisions that we make. We are the only people we can't lie to. We can make excuses and consolations all we want, but at the end of the day, we can't hide from what we know about ourselves. There is always an angel on the other shoulder waiting to tell us that there is a better way. If there is something we want to change, we have to say it out loud. Once we've done that, we can no longer pretend that we don't recognize the need for change, and more importantly, our desire for it.

You may be thinking, *People are always saying be nice to yourself, be kind to yourself, don't beat yourself up.* I am not saying you shouldn't give yourself some grace. There will always be things out of our control that affect us, and we can allow ourselves to reevaluate where we are at any given moment. However, giving ourselves grace and not being honest with ourselves, are two very different things.

The next chapter will kick off our journey to building a life we love from the bottom up, from start to never-ending finish, from nothing to all the things, and from where we are right now to where we want to be. But first, let's talk about the things that get in our way. There are more excuses than I can count, but the majority of them fit into these four categories: *I'll be happy when, I don't have any motivation, give yourself grace,* and *I don't have time.* Let's take a closer look at each of these.

I'll Be Happy When ...

I call this *a Mad Libs' excuse.*

When I _____ then
_____,

or

I'll be _____ when
_____.

There are a million different combinations of these phrases, just insert your words (here).

When I lose weight, then I'll feel confident enough to go on dates.

I'll be happy when I finally finish my thesis.

When I finish this project at work, then I'll be able to help my parents more.

I'll be happy when I am finally promoted and have a say in the way things are done.

When my kids graduate high school, then I'll have a life of my own.

Does any combination of these sound familiar?

By tying our happiness to what we accomplish, we are placing conditions on ourselves that keep our happiness just out of reach and continuously unattainable. We can't get the thing we want because we either never reach the goal, or we meet the goal, and there is another stipulation immediately put in place. This spiral keeps us from what we want ... or what we *think* we want. By giving ourselves an ultimatum to finish something before we can feel confident, successful, happy, fulfilled, or (*insert your word of choice here*), we are *choosing* to give our control over to yet another arbitrary goal.

Happiness and weight loss are not mutually exclusive.

Happiness and status are not mutually exclusive.

Happiness is not mutually exclusive with anything.

Happiness is a state of being.

It's possible to find happiness 100 percent of the time. It's a mindset that requires practice and an understanding of what it means to be happy. (We will discuss this further in chapter 7.)

Take a moment to think more deeply about how the following phrase makes you feel.

Your life won't wait for you.

I think about this phrase often when I am working out to an exercise video, and I need a moment to catch my breath. My natural instinct is to grab the remote and hit pause until I am ready to keep going. I remind myself that, unlike my ability to hit pause while exercising, I am not able to pause my life until I've had a moment to catch my breath. I struggle with perfectionism, so I don't want to miss out on anything; however, it is an opportunity to remind myself that it's OK if I miss a few things, it's OK that the experience is not perfect. I try to remember that, as long as I did the best I could, and I don't give up, I will have another opportunity to practice working through the physical and mental challenges of life without pressing pause. This practice strengthens me.

I also think about the statement *life won't wait for you* when I try to put a contingency in front of my happiness. The excuses we use are getting in the way of achieving what we truly want. Although they can be frustrating, our excuses can also be useful. They can help us to know ourselves better and become more aware of our thoughts. They give us an inside look at the desires of our hearts that whisper things like *Go on more dates. Finish school. Feel confident at work. Make more money. Have more authority. Have more time and freedom.* Do any of these sound familiar?

The grass is not always greener on the other side. Let's pretend that you get the promotion, which comes with a raise *and* more hours, more responsibility, and less freedom. Or you lose the weight you said you needed to lose before you could begin to date, but the guys/girls available are the same ones you dated before you reached your weight-loss goal.

When our happiness lies in reaching external goals, like a title, or a significant other, we place a contingency on the success that we should be celebrating. Let's shift the focus to celebrating your personal and professional development and the hard work that it took to get the promotion. Instead of celebrating the weight loss goal, can we celebrate the strength and dedication it took to lose the weight? The true benefits of reaching goals like getting stronger, getting promoted, reading a book, writing a book, etc. are not the external rewards, but the confidence and trust we build in ourselves through the process. If we can tie our happiness to our actions as opposed to the outcome, it creates an additional level of accountability to our daily effort and attitude.

This may feel hard. Shifting from an if/then to a this/and relationship with our goals is going to take time. We so often hear about filling our own cups first, or putting the oxygen mask on yourself first so you don't pass out before actually being able to help someone else, but what does that shift look like?

I think it's time we find out!

I Don't Have Any Motivation

We use this one a lot, at least I do. It is likely the most recognized and relatable excuse we use to explain why we don't finish (or even start) the things that we set out to do. If you've ever said *I don't have the motivation* out loud (I know I have), it feels so real in that moment. It is such a defeating and sometimes exhausting feeling that in the moment, it would never occur to us that we actually have power over it. There are a few things that cause this feeling and make it hard to overcome. The first is either not knowing *why* we're pursuing the goal in the first place or not having a strong enough intention toward the goal. We've all heard that in order to reach our goals, we have to have a clear understanding of *why* the goal is important and use that as fuel, even on the days we don't feel like it.

I don't disagree with this concept, but I do think it goes deeper than that. Our motivations change on a daily basis. Trying to overcome that with a singular reason *why* you set the goals won't work consistently. Starting a business, writing a book, eating healthier, finding more/better friends, exercising, reading personal development or reading more in general, becoming more flexible, working toward a promotion, having a deeper relationship with a spouse, etc. All of these goals can be worked on simultaneously, but they're not likely to all have the same *why*.

For example, you may have started a business or a side hustle to use your passion as a way to provide for your family. Or maybe you are writing a book, like I was, to tell your story and get your message out for those who need to hear it. You may be working to get healthier to feel self-confident and be more capable of playing with your kids or grandkids. You may be working toward a promotion so you can use all of the things you've learned to be a good leader while simultaneously making more money to provide for your family. For me, not only do I want to tell my story to help others, but I want to read more to have a stronger mindset and be more empathetic to other people's points of view. (I am working really hard to overcome my *"It's my way or the highway"* mentality.)

It's becoming more common to hear that you should focus more on discipline and less on motivation. (It's as easy as that, right?) But, I'm here to tell you that *motivation is not dead!* It is necessary. Let's take a deeper look at motivation. It is the feeling we get when we're not proud of what we see when we look in the mirror. That feeling motivates us to get in better shape so we can look better. We're motivated to eat healthier so we will feel better. When it comes to finances, motivation is the uncomfortable feeling we get when we're cutting it too close when paying our bills each month. We're motivated to work toward a promotion or get a second job. We're motivated to be more conscious about where we are spending our money and cutting back on spending.

Our goals are built on the motivation we feel when there is something in our lives that we want to change. I've led workshops where five people wanted to start exercising, all with a different *motivation* or *why*. If we discount motivation and rely simply on discipline, we're taking the personality and the individualization out of the goal and detaching from the original *why*, making it harder to succeed. Just as discounting the need for discipline, and simply relying on motivation, would be discouraging because we often lack the motivation we felt in the moment.

As important as it is, motivation is a feeling—it is fleeting. When our options at 8 p.m. are to exercise, or sit and watch TV with our spouse while we eat ice cream (it's a specific example for a reason!), the choice seems simple. In that situation, the *motivation* it would take to turn off the TV, change our clothes, put on our shoes, and get ready to workout seems like more than we have the energy for. This is when having a combination of discipline (doing what we say we're going to do, because we told ourselves we were going to do it), and motivation (our why) works.

We can tap back into that original feeling of motivation to help us through these roadblocks. The original moment that caused us to set the goal and the original conversation we had in our head about why setting this goal was going to make a difference in our lives are critical to access. We can also learn to ask better questions. Not, *Why is this so hard?* but *Why did I originally decide to set this goal? How can I channel that feeling and push through just this one time? Can I handle five minutes?* And a reminder that, *I can stop if I'm not into it.* Having these conversations with ourselves, and asking ourselves better questions, may help us to push past that uncomfortable feeling. With every conversation, every decision, and every action we put toward our goal, our discipline muscle grows stronger. And the next time, the conversation will likely be shorter, and the action to get up and start, will be a lot less taxing.

Sometimes it is really hard to make the choice that is better for you in the long run. (Does it ever occur to you that as an adult you have the choice to go out and buy an entire chocolate cake for supper? I know I've thought about it a time or two!) The process is hard, and it could defeat us, or it could excite us. What would it look like to have a conversation with ourselves about what we really want, what's really important, and what is going to get us to where we need to be? I encourage you to try it, and to remember former NFL player Michael Oher's words, "Excuses make today easy but they make tomorrow hard. Discipline makes today hard, but it makes tomorrow easy."[2] If we want to change our lives, we have to find a way; if not, we will find an excuse.

Give Yourself Grace

Giving ourselves grace is necessary; but it can also be an excuse. Let me explain.

I don't know that I have ever uttered this phrase or that it has ever occupied the confines of my mind. I have never tried to coach myself out of a problem and thought, *You need to give yourself some grace.* I am not typically that nice to myself. Before I started reading books about leadership and personal development, I would tell myself something along the lines of *Give up now; it's not worth it.* Now that I have become more self-aware, I say things like, *Push through it, Desiree. You're learning,* or *Progress happens daily, not in a day,*[3] which is an idea I learned from John Maxwell. Being able to give ourselves grace, without letting ourselves off the hook, is a skill that we have to learn. We are often our own worst critics. With all of that being said, I still don't think I've ever stopped and said to myself, *Give yourself grace, Desiree.*

Do you want to know when I typically hear the phrase, *Give yourself grace*? It's when one friend is trying to comfort another friend. (I am absolutely guilty of this too!) When we explain our struggles to someone who loves us, it's hard for that person to know what to say in response. It's probably frowned upon to say, *Stop whining and just do it!* or *You haven't succeeded because you don't try*! *Give yourself grace* feels like the appropriate response to give

---

[2]https://www.goodreads.com/quotes/11539002-excuses-make-today-easy-but-they-make-tomorrow-hard-discipline

[3] https://www.johnmaxwell.com/blog/leaders-develop-daily-not-in-a-day/

to someone who needs help, but what if what we need is something more?

How can we know what a friend needs from us? Is it advice, a compliment, or grace? Ask them!

Every time I am about to say, *Give yourself grace* to a friend who is confiding in me, I try to stop and ask some clarifying questions. The benefit of asking friends questions in return is that they may find they already know the answer. Sometimes asking a clarifying question helps to bring out answers they haven't yet allowed themselves to consider. Questions like: *Is this still where you want to be spending your time and energy, or is your heart in a different place now?* If they are upset about something someone said about them, I'll try to ask, *Is the opinion of this person who's criticizing you worth your worry? Or is it time to set a new boundary?* One of my favorite questions to ask my coaching clients is, *What advice would you give a friend right now if they were having this issue?* When I was a department head in a prior job, I would often ask, *Do you want to know what I think you could do, or do you want to just vent for a while?* Sometimes people just want to complain and not have to be rational. (I have read that there is no science proving that venting actually helps you to feel better, but I would have to heavily disagree!)

We can give people an opportunity to either come up with some constructive action steps to better the situation themselves or simply allow them to get it off their chest so they know they're not alone, which helps create some stability for them. The hope is that asking better questions and trying to help them through the situation, as opposed to around it, will help you to avoid letting them off the hook. We can dig a bit deeper and let them be the judge of where they could best use our support. Assure the people coming to you that they have the ability to do whatever it is they want to do. Ask if you can be of assistance in some way. Provide advice if they want it. Ask if they want some tough love, or if they need you to be kind.

If you close your eyes and try to picture how this conversation would go, you may think it would be incredibly awkward and choppy. But let's turn the roles around. What if the next time we wanted to give up on our exercise goals, someone asked us how they could help or encouraged us by saying that we can do anything we put our mind to. What if the next time we wanted to give up on our dream of owning our own business, a friend gave us permission to use *Give yourself grace* as an excuse not to continue. We might feel that we were right to question if we could do it because of all of the obstacles in our way and give up on the spot. What if instead our friend asked us a question like, *Why did you start this business*? While answering the question, we may realize that our motivation got lost along the way. Asking—or being asked—the better questions may rekindle a fire we thought had long since burnt out.

What if the next time we told a friend that we felt like a bad spouse or parent, that friend complimented the ways we are an amazing spouse or parent. What if that friend offered to help and gave us some advice about what has worked for him or her. Doing this reminds us of how amazing we are and how hard we try to be everything to everyone! It reminds us that we're not alone in our feelings, and we have support and tools to make the situation better.

I do believe there are times we need to give ourselves grace, but it's a fine line between giving ourselves wiggle room to reevaluate what we want and who we want to be and giving ourselves an excuse to give up on our goals and dreams.

Next time you're told to *give yourself grace*, ask yourself if that's what you really need. Don't be afraid to dig a bit deeper, you already know the answer! Sometimes we just need to find the courage to ask the right questions to be a good friend to ourselves and others.

I Don't Have Time

We all have different priorities that take up different amounts of time. Some of mine may seem absolutely ridiculous to you and like a waste of time, and I may not relate to yours. We may have hobbies, spouses, children, and other needs that take different amounts of time between various interests and activities. Some people may not have any kids, or they're already out of the home. Some have parents that require a lot of time and attention as they age. Some people work part-time, some work 40 hours a week, and some may work 80+ hours.

Not having time is a matter of misunderstanding our priorities, rather than an actual measurement of free time. Overcoming the challenge, or rather the *excuse* of not having enough time is simple, but not always easy.

The moment we say that we don't have enough time to do the things that we *say* we want, we give up all of the potential to conquer the lack of time and figure out how to fit our priorities into 24 hours. In other words, we've already signaled to our minds that there is no further discussion on the matter.

I have had to change my goals over the years to fit into the reality of my time. When my daughter was born, I was reading 100 books a year; by the time my son was born, I had to cut back to 60. Now that I am a year into my business, I am realizing that my goal is more overwhelming than inspiring. I don't have time, that is the fact, but if I said that aloud, my immediate thought as a perfectionist would be to stop reading. Instead, I have had to ask myself a few questions, like *How many books is reasonable to read in a year with everything I've got going on? Do I want it to be a stretch goal, where I likely won't reach my goal, but I'll read more knowing that I was trying to get to a bigger number, or do I want a win? In which case, I can set the goal lower so I know I can actually hit it.* I don't want to change my goal. I take pride in being able to read as much as I do, and not only that, but I *love* to read. I don't want to give up on that. So instead of saying I don't have time (which I don't), I am asking myself a few questions to stay creative and find a way to make sure that I can keep reading as a priority, just on different terms.

(For a list of all of my favorite books [including fiction, memoirs, personal development, etc.], visit desireepetrich.com/books.)

If something is not a priority in this season of life, that's OK! If we find ourselves feeling guilty day after day that we can't fit something into our schedule, we need to ask ourselves a few questions to determine if it is really that important in the current season. If we come to the conclusion that it's not a priority, replace it with something that is. We have the option to take the weight off of our own shoulders. If we decide it is a priority, we can redefine what it would look like to successfully reach that goal (we will dive deeper into this in chapter five).

When we evaluate these time excuses, we take back our power and control. Excuses come in all shapes and sizes, but being able to recognize them will help us get to know ourselves better. We will be more effective with the things we can control, and we'll learn lessons and gain strength from the circumstances we can't.

Someone once told me that one of his core values is the ability to *eliminate* the excuses that stand between him and his goals. I am not willing to write off excuses that easily. I believe that our excuses have a story to tell. They help us understand and shift our priorities during different seasons of our lives. We can learn when to make things a priority, when to put things on the backburner, or when to throw them out entirely. Learning to evaluate our excuses allows us to make informed decisions about our lives and the direction we're choosing to take. We get to set goals for ourselves, learn how to reach them, and learn when to let them go. We get to ask ourselves important questions to evaluate our priorities and what stands in the way of achieving them. We get to bring people into our lives that are able to help us see the truth behind our excuses. We have the choice to not only survive but to thrive!

CHAPTER 2: CHOOSING TO THRIVE

"Forces beyond your control **can** take away everything you possess except one thing, your freedom to <u>choose</u> how you **will** respond to the situation."[4]
- Viktor Frankl
(The emphasis here is mine.)

There is one more excuse that needs to be discussed—*You only live once*—or YOLO. *You only live once* is a phrase that can be traced back to 1993 in a trademark filed for YOLO gear with "you only live once" printed across the front of a T-shirt.[5] However, most people would recognize the phrase from 2011 when the rapper, Drake, used the phrase in his song "The Motto."[6] (Here is where I would typically insert the lyrics, but you don't realize how inappropriate they are until you read them word for word!) From there, the acronym was entered into the Oxford English Dictionary in 2016 and has been a common phrase used ever since.[7]

I really struggle with this excuse, because too often, I see people use this phrase to justify doing stupid things.

---

[4]https://quotefancy.com/quote/384664/Viktor-E-Frankl-Forces-beyond-your-control-can-take-away-everything-you-possess-except
[5] https://trademarks.justia.com/877/64/yolo-87764836.html
[6] https://www.forbes.com/sites/leorgalil/2012/12/29/does-drake-own-yolo/?sh=460935c42556
[7] https://www.oed.com/dictionary/yolo_int?tl=true&tab=factsheet

Why can't I drink myself into oblivion and have a good time doing it? YOLO!

I have $100 I was saving to put toward something important, but I really want this pair of shoes that I'll probably never wear. YOLO!

Yes, I have been trying really hard to lose weight, but I want to eat this entire plate of cookies, and I can start again tomorrow. YOLO!

The issue I have with this phrase is that it gives us an excuse to give in to the easier choice in the moment, and we end up abandoning our commitment to intentional choice and reaching our longer term goal. If you've set a goal for yourself to stay sober, save money, go to bed earlier, try to get healthier, etc., those choices were not made lightly. The choice to set a goal is sometimes viewed as a spur of the moment decision, but often the goal has simply been unspoken up until that point. Just because we hadn't said it out loud to that point doesn't mean it hasn't been on our hearts and in our heads for a long time. The decision to set a goal should hold some merit and give us strength when faced with things that may feel good in the moment.

We are living in a unique time as a society. We are in the first age of social media and only at the very beginnings of seeing its longer-term effects. Social media's emphasis on images and trends creates a lot of pressure to live a life that looks good to people on the outside. If we don't feel like we are living up to others' expectations, it's really easy to give up on our goals. This may be because of situational pressure to do whatever is *on trend* or a belief that hitting our goals is going to be too hard.

Excuses are choices too, and there is nothing wrong with that. In her book, *Chasing the Bright Side,* Jess Ekstrom says that

"Telling yourself you can quit at any moment isn't a reminder of weakness; it's a reminder of choice. And when we choose to keep going, we're choosing to recommit to our purpose."[8]

When we give in to situational pressure or make a decision because we're scared not to, that's not making a choice. Making a choice looks like weighing all of the options. It looks like giving yourself the right amount of time to make sure you've thought the decision through, and you won't have to look back with any sort of regret or guilt later.

This may sound like I am referring to life-changing choices, like whether to have more children, move your family to pursue a new career, or buy a house with a mortgage you're not sure you can afford, even though you *really* love it. But the choices I'm talking about are on a much smaller scale. We make a lot of decisions throughout the day. How can we make sure that we aren't taking any of those decisions for granted without giving them the proper consideration? The answer is *conditional permission*. Conditional permission is a tool I use to make better decisions, without feeling like my option to choose has been taken away. It's based on the understanding that we are all adults with the right to choose what we do and don't do, while also understanding that the consequences of that decision, good or bad, are also our responsibility. Conditional permission simply creates a pocket of time for you to contemplate your options and make the best decision you can in the moment. You give yourself permission to do anything you want, but with one condition that has to be met before you can access full permission. Wake up with your alarm, exercise, read, say no to sweets and treats. All of these goals can be mastered once you've given yourself conditional permission.

---

[8] Jess Ekstrom, *Chasing The Bright Side*, (Tennessee: W Publishing, 2019), 84.

In the following example, I will break down what it looks like to create conditional permission around waking up early. Part one is getting out of bed when my alarm goes off, while using the snooze button as a tool as opposed to an obstacle. Part two outlines the condition. I am an adult, I can go back to bed if that's what I choose to do, but first, I create a condition for myself that allows for enough time to weigh my decisions before deciding to either get up for the day, or go back to bed.

In this example, the first part of this tool is to simply get out of bed.

Step one: Put your phone in another room. Although not groundbreaking advice, I will remind you that if your goal is to go to bed earlier, read more, do less social media scrolling, or create more time to connect with a spouse, this one habit will immediately put you in a better position to reach all of those goals!

Step two: If you have a Fitbit, Apple watch, or any other type of wearable device, make sure you wear it to bed. If your alarm clock on your watch is connected to the alarm on your phone, you'll need to download a separate alarm app on your phone so you aren't able to turn off your alarm from your watch.

Step three: Set your phone alarm to the time you want to wake up. (Find an outlet outside of your bedroom to plug it in.) Set your watch alarm, or a good old fashioned bedside alarm to six minutes before your phone alarm. The idea here is that you will be able to hit the snooze button, knowing that you have to get up and turn off the alarm in the other room, before it goes off and wakes up others in your house.

(I struggled with this part. I liked knowing that I had a built-in snooze button that I could hit, but six minutes was too long to give myself before I had to get up and turn off my phone alarm. I would fall back asleep and then get startled awake when my alarm would go off in the other room. This was not the goal!)

Step four: Set a second alarm on your watch or bedside alarm clock three minutes before your final alarm will go off.

The first alarm is to wake you up and encourage you to hit the snooze button. Give yourself that three minutes to do whatever feels best. You can use the time to drift back to sleep, pray, start a gratitude practice, whatever works best for you. You officially have a built-in three minutes to enjoy the snooze button. It doesn't seem like much, but it makes a huge difference when you eliminate the dreaded feeling of having to get up with your alarm (at least not the first one!).

When your second alarm goes off, this is your cue. You officially have three minutes to get out of bed, get to your phone, and turn off the alarm before it goes off.

Pro tip: pick the loudest, most obnoxious alarm on your phone. The ultimate goal is that you will never have to hear it!

I know that seems like a lot of instructions, but I promise you, the repetition will condition your mind to the process, and it will begin to get easier and easier to get up and turn off the final alarm before it goes off.

As I began to master the process of getting out of bed, I was experiencing a secondary problem. I still had to convince myself to stay out of bed once the alarm was off. It was still too easy to crawl back into bed and fall back asleep. I realized that some days I did truly need to go back to sleep, whether my kids were up a lot during the night, my body was exhausted from a tough workout, or I just didn't sleep well the night before. Some days I actually needed to get back into bed and get more sleep. Most days, though, I was crawling back into bed because it was the easier option, especially at 5 a.m.

To give myself enough time to truly think through whether or not I needed to go back to sleep, I had to ask myself if additional sleep was really necessary. I needed to find some time to make those decisions, this is where the condition came in. I gave myself permission to go back to sleep, but I first had to wash my face with cold water and brush my teeth. If I still felt like I needed more sleep after completing those tasks, I gave myself permission to go back to bed. By placing the condition in front of the permission, I was giving myself just enough time to think through my options, tap back into my original motivation for setting the goal, and make the best decision. If you wake up at 5 a.m. but have nothing to do, there is very little reason to stay out of bed. If you wake up at 5 a.m. to read a book, exercise, work on a project, drink your coffee in peace, or take a sunrise walk, you have a much more compelling reason to stay out of bed and start your day.

Here's the thing, we're not wrong. Regardless of the option we choose, as long as we give ourselves enough time to think about the choices we make, we won't be wrong. We may end up with consequences we don't like, such as missing those five minutes of peace in the morning or having to jog in place at 9 p.m. to get all of our 10,000 steps in before bed (that example is specific for a reason), but you will learn from that decision. We can bring back that feeling the next time we're trying to decide whether to stay awake or go back to bed.

With every decision we make toward our goals, we are giving ourselves the opportunity to trust the decisions we make. We have to find ways to give ourselves conditional permission. This helps build a level of consistency because it takes perfectionism out of the equation. We are making decisions in the moment, not out of impulse, but with a set of questions to make sure we're making the right decision in that moment.

We are capable of making good decisions and exercising choice; however, YOLO is not a good strategy for making healthy decisions. We must understand that not choosing is still a choice, and we can begin to give ourselves the credit we deserve every time we make a choice that's best for us.

Willpower versus Reason

I am never one to back down from a challenge. To say I'm competitive may be an understatement. However, I don't care if someone else beats me (Yay for them!) but I don't want to be beaten by my own inability to follow through on what I say I'm going to do. Some of this comes from my desire to be in control, but ever since I gave up pop and began exercising and reading consistently, people have called me *disciplined*. Once you've taken that label on, you feel the pressure to live up to it. It's hard to think you may not be able to anymore.

I have started the 75 Hard Challenge twice now. It is a "transformative mental toughness program" created by entrepreneur Andy Frisella in 2019.[9] The first time I attempted it, I was trying to lose the last 20 pounds of baby weight I was still carrying after my second baby. I was 21 days into the challenge and felt *amazing*! Below are the daily requirements for some perspective.

75 Hard Challenge

- Two 45 minute workouts (one must be outdoors)
- Pick a nutrition plan (no alcohol and no cheating)

---

[9] https://www.forbes.com/health/fitness/what-is-the-75-hard-challenge/

- Read ten pages of a personal development book
- Drink one gallon of water a day
- Take one selfie as a progress photo every day

The challenge is to do each of these things every day for 75 Days. If you cheat, you have to start over.

My husband and I had plans to spend a weekend away with our best friends—no kids—and the overall goal was to have a good time. I knew that we had this trip coming when I decided to start 75 Hard, but as a *disciplined* person, I was convinced I could stick to the rules. There was no way I was starting over when I was almost a third of the way done! For the two weeks leading up to the trip I debated whether I should continue the 75 Hard Challenge or if I should quit and start again when I got home. How was I going to get two 45-minute workouts every day? The time commitment made me nervous, but my biggest concern was sticking to a diet. I had high hopes that my willpower would come through and save me in the hard times. I continued to remind myself of the goal that I had set and how great I had been feeling for the past three weeks. I told my husband and friends about my plan to stick to the rules but assured them it wouldn't interfere with their fun!

Then we made our first stop: Minnesota's Largest Candy Store. Now, before you question what kind of friends would bring you to a candy store when you're trying not to eat sweets, they did offer to skip this stop. But who wouldn't want to go to a candy store? Besides, I'm apparently a glutton for punishment and like to torture myself just to prove I am strong!

Believe it or not, I made it through that entire store without purchasing a single item—talk about willpower! I also made it through the next hour of our drive while the other three enjoyed their candy and reminisced about the experience. I continued to be in good spirits without complaining. After three weeks of no sugar,

I wasn't craving it too badly, but I was now realizing the next four days might be harder than I had originally thought.

Then we made our next stop: the liquor store right down the street from our rental house. I don't typically drink other than on special occasions, but I was starting to feel like I was a prude—unable to enjoy myself for an entire four days because I was focused on sticking to this arbitrary set of rules. At this point, I began to question my motives for the goals that I had set for myself. I wanted to lose some weight. I wanted to feel better in my clothes and maybe put on some extra muscle. I wanted to spend more time outside and the required outdoor workouts were helping in that sense. Couldn't I accomplish these goals and still enjoy a weekend with my friends?

This was not a YOLO decision. I didn't choose to break my 21-day streak on a whim or because I felt pressured into it. My husband and friends never said a word about my decision to opt out of some of the activities for the weekend. I explained it to them, and there were no questions asked. So, what was the decision based on? A choice—my choice.

I analyzed my goals. I recognized that giving myself the option to quit wasn't a sign of weakness but a reminder that I had a choice. A choice to recommit to my goal of losing weight, or a choice to indulge for the weekend and have to *start over on Monday.* I ultimately decided on a compromise and landed somewhere in the middle. I didn't have to quit and start over on Monday. I decided to give myself a little extra wiggle room. My goals were still at the forefront of my mind. Losing weight and gaining muscle was still important to me. We still went on one, if not two, hikes every day. I woke up early and got in 45 minutes of yoga while everyone else was still sleeping. I still attempted to keep my alcohol and sugar intake to a minimum. I still read personal development books out in the hammock and before going to bed.

The all-or-nothing mentality and YOLO attitude go hand in hand. Throwing your hands up and saying *YOLO* is an excuse, but it's also a choice. You don't have to be all in or all out. You know yourself well enough that you can make engaged and informed decisions about the way you choose to spend your time and your money. You can choose to spend time with people that inspire you and push you to stick to your goals, as opposed to those who will encourage you to give up on everything you have been working toward because ... *YOLO!*

When we returned home from our vacation, I was feeling a mix of pride and frustration. I was proud of myself for not going 180 degrees in the opposite direction; I was proud of myself that I was able to still fit in most of my non-negotiable habits. Ultimately, I was proud that my *perfectionist, all-or-nothing* mindset hadn't won. I had managed to end up somewhere in the middle. On the other hand, I was frustrated that I would now have to start over again.

The second time I started the 75 Hard Challenge was because I wanted to prove to myself that I could do it. Everyone looked at me as a disciplined person, and I wanted to prove them right. It had been a month since the last time I attempted the challenge. I hadn't given up on my goals. I was still exercising and attempting to stick to a diet. I was still drinking a lot of water, and reading a lot. It wouldn't be that hard, right? I lasted six days. Even the most disciplined and dedicated individuals cannot follow through on a goal if it's not for the right reasons.

As we continue to revisit the goals that we have set for ourselves, we can't be afraid to change them, increase or decrease them, or even cross them off the list. The important thing to remember is that our choices should be based on a deep understanding of ourselves and our motivations behind why we set the goal in the first place.

Choosing When It Feels Like There Is No Choice

On February 21, 2022, at 10 a.m. I got a call from my nurse that I needed to be induced within the next 24 hours if I didn't want to risk having a stillborn baby. The bloodwork that they had taken five days prior, (due to my complaint about waking up with itchy hands), came back positive for cholestasis, a liver problem that slows or stops the normal flow of bile from the gallbladder.[10] I was only one week from my due date so they weren't concerned about development, but they were concerned about the effect this condition could have on my baby. So, we quickly packed my pillow and a hospital bag (because, unlike a good Boy Scout, I am *not* always prepared) and headed to the hospital.

When I had my first baby in 2019, my mom was by my side. This time, the new COVID-19 policies prevented her from being in the room. She offered to come to the hospital and sit in the parking lot, but with some bad weather on the way, we decided she needed to stay home. I had my son less than 12 hours after being induced. He was born at 1:44 a.m. (We had some bets going with the medical staff that he would be born at 2:22 a.m. on 2/22/22. We were only 38 minutes off!) He was perfect. My husband and I couldn't get over how cute his little grunts were—he was already talking to us! Turns out, the nurse didn't feel the same. Only ten minutes after having him placed in my arms, he was being taken out of them again. They wanted to do some additional testing because he should have stopped gasping for air by this point. Turns out I had him too quickly. He didn't have enough time in the birth canal to do what God created the process of childbirth to do. His left lung hadn't had time to expand. Typically, this wouldn't be such a problem. The NICU staff from another hospital (this is where you should go back

---

[10] https://my.clevelandclinic.org/health/diseases/17901-cholestasis-of-pregnancy

and read the introduction if you haven't already!) would fly the helicopter (air ambulance) the 85 miles to the hospital we were in, pick up our baby, and take him to a place that could take care of him. Unfortunately, in true Minnesota fashion, there was a blizzard that made it impossible for any helicopters, fixed-winged airplanes, or ambulances to get to us.

There were 15 people in the nursery with our son. My husband and I were not included.

The pediatrician canceled the rest of his schedule to come sit next to our son (who at this point still did not have a name). The only respiratory therapist canceled her schedule to sit and manually respirate him. Unfortunately, the hospital did not have the equipment to intubate a baby. Unlike 2019, when our daughter was baby number 18 out of 19 babies born in 3 days, our son was the only baby on the delivery floor that day. We had every nurse in the room with him. The NICU team from 85 miles away was on telehealth with a video camera monitoring him and instructing the staff on what to do next. He needed a drug to create space in his lungs, but the hospital only had half of the dose needed. (He was over eight pounds, and typically babies born at full term wouldn't need this type of medication.) An ambulance driver from our hospital drove 23 miles in the opposite direction of the NICU and away from the storm—to meet an ambulance from another hospital to get the other half of the needed medication.

Through all of the twists and turns, it felt like days were going by, when in all reality, it hadn't even been 12 hours. The funny thing is, I don't remember being afraid. I don't recall ever questioning if he was going to be OK.

One of my least favorite (and favorite) things about my husband is that he stays calm ... always. He is a glass-half-full individual to the point it gets extremely annoying. If I complain about anything, he always responds, "It could be worse." So, in this scenario, when I said aloud what I was thinking, such as, "Why is this happening? What did I do wrong? Why does this have to be so hard?" he said, "At least this problem can be fixed."

By hour 15, our son was on the way to the NICU on a fixed-wing plane, with more medical concerns than he started with and not yet out of the woods. Little did we know that we had almost four more weeks to go. It's so easy in situations that are out of our control to have a woe-is-me attitude. It's easy to question why bad things are always happening *to you*. By giving our power over to the things that are out of our control, we are choosing to let those things win. We are making an *excuse* and giving up the things we do have power over to focus on the things we don't.

Within 24 hours of having a baby, I was no longer able to claim the identity of someone who had just given birth. I had new and immediate responsibilities I never could have anticipated. I was now responsible for finding a place to stay while our infant was in the NICU. I was responsible for figuring out who was going to watch our two-year-old daughter when she had never spent more than a day with anyone but Mom and/or Dad. I had to walk three-quarters of a mile from our hotel to my baby's room on the fourth floor of the hospital, multiple times a day. I thanked God daily for the fact that after giving birth I had the physical ability to walk that far, or at all. I had to decide if I was going to pump every three hours even though my baby wouldn't be able to use any of the milk for a few weeks because he was being fed through a tube down his throat.

These things alone could have had the power to break every habit I had spent the last three years building. The stress of the situation would have been an excuse that no one could have argued with me about. But my husband's voice kept saying, *It could be worse*. If you've ever known anyone like this, you may ask how I avoided punching him ... and I would tell you that I came close on more than one occasion!

Sometimes you just want to complain ... and cry ... and yell. Anything to make yourself feel better. Anything to not have to be the responsible one *all the time*. But having someone to remind you that it could be worse, helps keep things in perspective. Eventually, that voice starts to sound a lot more like your own, and you begin to view things with a new lens. When you view things with the glass being at least half full, you learn to not only work through the stress and the pain; you can sometimes even learn to laugh through it and be the strong one in times of overwhelming pain. You never know when the skills to be optimistic and realistic at the same time will save your sanity.

I am so far from perfect. You better believe that I ate a free donut from the hotel lobby almost every morning. We used every meal voucher that the hospital gave us for the hospital cafeteria (surprisingly, the food wasn't too bad!). But there were old habits that pulled me through all of the chaos, and helped me to work through the long days and nights, especially the nights I was there alone because my husband went home to be with our daughter.

Some of the things I was able to keep control of during this time were:

- Reading. I had a goal to read 75 books that year. I spent most of my days reading or listening to a book, while I sat in his room unable to hold my baby until he was extubated.

- Stretching. I had a goal to stretch at least 20 minutes every night, and knew I would feel better if I did at least that much. (I got quite a few strange looks from the nursing staff when they'd walk past our room to find me on the floor stretching just a few days after giving birth.)

- Practicing Gratitude. James (my husband) and I were in total agreement that we needed to make sure the hospital staff knew how much we appreciated their time and care. We always kept the candy bucket in our room full. Every few days we would buy a laundry basket full of chips, sparkling water, and granola bars to have delivered to the nurses' station. We tried not only to show our appreciation but to make sure we voiced our gratitude to the staff.

- Trusting. There were times that decisions had to be made, and we had to put 100 percent of our faith into the staff caring for our infant. This usually isn't hard for me. Most of the time I feel I am naive to the severity of situations, and I choose to leave the decision to those with the most knowledge.

  My mom taught me this. She didn't love to fly, but she would always make herself feel better by saying, "The pilot wants to make it home as badly as I do, and he will do what he needs to do to get us there." My husband and I used this mentality to remind ourselves that the doctors and nurses wanted to see our son healthy and ready to go home to his sister just as much as we did. There was never a doubt in my mind that they would make the right decisions to get us closer to that day.

- Maintaining Levity. Two weeks into our stay, we decided it would be fun to have our daughter join us for the weekend in our hotel. We went swimming at the hotel with my mom and sisters. My mom bought our daughter some blocks to keep her busy in the hotel, and we got James's favorite Papa John's pizza to eat on the floor of the hotel room. It was then that we saw the bug ... a bedbug.

I won't lie and say that we didn't have a few moments of *Why us?* and *Are you serious?* thoughts between us. But, ultimately, we decided to be thankful for the situation and laugh at how ridiculous it was! Let me explain, after multiple weeks of living in the hotel, our hotel room had become a mess with clothes everywhere and snacks piled high. Moments after we saw the bug, we started the process of washing all of our clothes in the hotel laundry room and changing rooms (Yes, we decided to stay in the hotel. The location across from the hospital was too good to give up!) Through the exhaustion and disbelief that we were in the situation, it occurred to me that I hadn't been home in over two weeks. I had been having James bring me clothes as I needed them, (which meant that I had 12 pairs of socks and no clean shirts). We were halfway through the process of cleaning our room, when we decided to make the 90 minute drive home to reset and repack. I only got to be home for nine hours because I had to be back the next morning for rounds. But oh my goodness, I can't explain to you how nice it was to use my own shampoo and sleep in my own bed! We chose to laugh at the situation and be thankful for the opportunity to go home.

- Increasing Faith. I put this one last only because everything that we do comes right back to this, our faith in God. Everything I had been through in my life up to this point was in preparation for the situation we had found ourselves in. I was able to stay calm and communicate with kindness and patience as a result of all of the personal development and communication work I had done. My struggles with PCOS (polycystic ovary syndrome) and not knowing if I would be able to have kids helped me stay grateful and be amazed at how hard my son was fighting.

This may be an unpopular opinion, but I don't believe the saying, *If it's meant to happen, it will happen.* I cringe when this phrase is used because it's an excuse like any other. It's an excuse to allow things to happen *to* us as opposed to taking control and working hard to get the things we want.

I do, however, believe that everything happens for a reason. "'For I know the plans I have for you,' declares the LORD, 'plans to prosper you and not to harm you, plans to give you hope and a future.'" (Jeremiah 29:11, NIV). God gives us opportunities to make decisions. The forks in the road are to exercise our free will. The harder or less traveled path won't necessarily bring a different outcome, but it may give you the tools to navigate your destination with more grace, patience, understanding, and strength.

Leaving a Legacy

In our hometown of Marshall, Minn., a family started a nonprofit organization called Squeeze The Stuffins. They did this to create a legacy for their son Reed after he passed in a horrific school bus accident. They had two other children in the accident as well. One of whom was fighting to live in the same hospital where Reed passed away in. The family wanted to give back to the hospital that was so kind and gentle to them during this impossible time.

They never wanted his tragic death to be his biggest headline; they wanted to celebrate the way that Reed loved others. They decided they wanted to give comfort to other grieving children when they were finally able to leave the hospital nine days after the bus crash. They were going home as two grieving parents, to two amazing but grieving children. The family now gives a stuffed cheetah (they were Reed's favorite animal), to the surviving siblings of any child who has passed away in that hospital.

I know this story well, because I have multiple stuffed animals from different fundraising events. They host the events to make sure every grieving child at this same hospital gets a Reed-a-Cheetah to *squeeze the stuffins* out of when they need a hug. This story became even more significant to me during my son's stay in that same hospital. A few weeks into our stay at the NICU, a set of twins were brought in. They were so small. In addition to the prayers we prayed for our son, we added the twins to what seemed like a never ending list of prayers. A few days later, one of the babies was gone, and in their place, sat a chair with a Cheetah perched next to the baby still fighting hard to stay in this world. I don't know if that baby survived as a twinless-twin, or if they are both in heaven with their arms wrapped tightly around one another. But I do know that the family had more love and prayers than they even knew, if only from my family and Reed's.

Reed's family chose to create a legacy. They had no control over the situation, but they did have control over the choices that were made in the aftermath. Many years later, I had the opportunity to hear Reed's mom speak. She told the story of her journey to forgive the woman who had caused the bus accident. This was a choice—a choice that was made out of the family's intent to love people, to give them grace, and to provide a safe place for college kids to call home when they were too far from their own. She found a way to show compassion and understanding. No one would have faulted their family for choosing to stay angry. From the outside looking in, it seems like anger is the choice most people would make.

When I reached out to Reed's mom to get permission to share their family's story, she said they would be honored. She also shared this, "We never give the cheetahs to receive any thanks or recognition from the families, and yet, families find us. The letters, cards, and calls we have received have deeply touched us, and they encourage us that what we have chosen as Reed's legacy is impacting lives. That is something for which he would be so proud."

There will always be circumstances out of our control. But building a foundation of resilience in your life can keep you steady. Resilience is "an ability to recover from or adjust easily to misfortune or change."[11] And resilience is not something that you either have or don't; it's something that you get to build. I heard that an individual can return to around 80 percent of the happiness level they were at before a tragedy, within one year. I can't remember where I heard this, but regardless of how accurate it is, the concept is extremely comforting and possibly even motivating if you choose to look at it as an opportunity. To me, this means that it's within our control to be happy and thankful in any given moment. You can build this foundation one day at a time, and you can choose to strengthen it by putting in the work every day. It's our choice to create a life that we are proud to be living. Regardless of the things we face, we can learn to be resilient by intentionally building a strong foundation.

---

[11] https://www.merriam-webster.com/dictionary/resilience

Chapter 3: Learning to Lead by Example

"If your actions create a legacy that inspires others to dream more, learn more, do more and become more, then, you are an excellent leader."[12]
- Dolly Parton

Dance, tennis, volleyball, golf, and track and field. These are just a few of the sports I attempted in high school. I was never considered great at any of them. I don't know if this is a thing everywhere, but where I lived, having the right last name had a lot to do with whether you got a chance to play or not (at least that's what you tell yourself when you're 15 and sitting on the bench). I never felt like I had the time or the opportunity to truly fall in love with any sport.

As an adult, I tried Herbalife, LulaRoe, Pampered Chef, Zyia, and Beachbody. These are just a few of the companies I either attempted to start side hustles in or at least got really close to starting. I always admired people having success in these ventures, and I wanted to be known for something too. I wanted to be the person who could make money doing something that I loved,

---

[12]https://www.goodhousekeeping.com/life/g38335193/strong-women-quotes/?utm_source=google&utm_medium=cpc&utm_campaign=arb_g a_ghk_md_dsa_prog_org_us_g38335193&gad_source=1&gclid=CjwKC Ajwz42xBhB9EiwA48pT7zGaFC7QLVxjqsxTMI4_HcxNAXMVXV2qzADc wM09u_KPH_Hl-ZlhrBoCekkQAvD_BwE

especially because other people had proven it was possible. So, why was it so hard for me?

I'm guessing you can relate to one of these examples, at least a little. My coaching clients are often looking for their passion or to understand what their purpose is in life. What they're really looking for is something they're good at, something they love, and something that can make them money. It's a hard combination, especially because we are expected to diversify and not be just an employee, parent, and friend anymore. We are conditioned to want more and to have a desire to be good at it. (Thank you, social media!)

The hard part is getting to where we can do what we love, make money, and be happy, all at the same time. It is an obscure combination of things that doesn't feel attainable by most people because there isn't one clear map to follow. At the age of 25, I had given up on this dream for myself. I had tried all the things and felt like finding my purpose and passion was just not something I was going to experience. At that point, I was willing to be an employee, do a really good job, and complete the tasks I was given. I may or may not have been over the moon with joy at any given moment, but at least I wasn't miserable thinking there was more out there for me but just out of reach. I had given up on that vision for my life.

It may seem like there is a big gap in the story between the 25-year-old who had completely given up dreaming and the 30-year-old who started and is running a successful leadership development company. That gap was made up of a combination of really small choices and large life events. Some of which were in my control and some that weren't. But when you're given lemons, you are given the choice to make lemonade. If you were to ask me today, I would tell you that almost every big event in my life has happened as a result of good and bad leadership, largely because hindsight is twenty-

twenty, but also because expanding the definition of leadership has opened my eyes to the influence of different leaders in our lives.

Leadership is one of those concepts that has evolved over time. Some will tell you that a leader is a manager of people; they have the upper hand because they have the position. Some may tell you that a leader is someone who makes the most money and therefore has the most power. Some may tell you that it's the person who influences the majority of people to do their bidding, regardless of how ethical the work is (think Hitler and Stalin).

None of these people are wrong. Leadership is more than one thing, more than just respect, trust, influence, power, the upper hand, and control. Leading is also no longer just about the workplace. Leading is about your ability to gain trust and respect and to have influence because you lead by example. You may even have the power or the upper hand, but you use it in a way that it benefits the greater good. You can be a confident leader at work, at home, at church, in your community, in your friendships, with your children, and everything in between. Leadership is knowing, trusting, inspiring, encouraging, and lifting up those around you to be better than they are right now. It's about believing in people, even when they don't believe in themselves.

Personal Leadership

I was not a fan of high school. By the time I started ninth grade, it was my third school, and I just wanted to blend in. I was friends with everyone but best friends with no one. I got As because the work was easy, not because I had to try hard. I worked in a nursing home 90 percent of the time I was not at school because I wanted to be responsible and provide for myself. (Not because my parents didn't, but because I wanted to be in control of the things that I purchased.) By the time I finished my junior year in high school, I was over it. I didn't want to be there anymore. I wanted to start my life and just go to college already.

I was qualified for post-secondary enrollment options, and instead of attending my senior year in high school, I started yet another new school and took college classes in a nearby town. This was my first taste of absolute freedom, and to be honest ... I kind of blew it! I didn't join any clubs or intramural sports. I didn't party on the weekends or go to sporting events. I did my schoolwork, went to the gym, and worked my part-time job. I was the somewhat shy person in the corner, who all of a sudden had to actually work for my grades. The easy As were starting to look more like Bs, and even a few Cs. I didn't enjoy my job as a home health aide, but I had been in healthcare since I started as a nursing assistant at age 15, I didn't know anything else. Needless to say, the amazing experience that I rushed out of high school for still wasn't meeting my expectations. In hindsight, I realize it's because I wasn't doing anything differently. I was following the exact same pattern and expecting different results. (I'm pretty certain that's the definition of insanity!)

I truly assumed that by changing the environment and the circumstances I was in, it would improve my situation. I assumed that grades would be easy like they always had been for me, but without the familiar students and teachers around me, I struggled to make friends and bond with my teachers. I didn't love my job, but I did love the people I got to help. I was comfortable in my disappointment, and it felt like too much work to change. It was easier to just complain about it. This was my first lesson in personal leadership. When we're in the middle of a lesson, it feels uncomfortable and sometimes hopeless, but it's just part of the journey. Working through these difficult times gets us closer to what we're searching for in our lives.

In 2017 (at the age of 24), I was waitressing at a local restaurant. At this point, I would have told anyone who asked that college is an absolute waste of time and money. I had gone to four years of school and had a business management degree, but no one would hire me because I didn't have experience. The thought constantly going through my head was, *How are you supposed to get experience if no one will hire you*? The ironic thing is that I don't think I had gone on more than two interviews. We are so quick to speak in absolutes about the things in our lives, like, *I never have time to read*, when you spend at least two hours a day watching TV. *This will never get any easier*, when you've only dedicated 20 hours to your new hobby. Or in my case, *No one will hire me*, when I had only applied to two jobs.

When we find ourselves saying the words *always* and *never*, we have to recognize that absolutes are an excuse! Typically, this type of excuse is subconscious. We truly believe that *never* and *always* are the correct amount of time associated with what we want. Our fear of stepping out of our comfort zone or taking responsibility for something that isn't a guarantee can cause us to feel like what we want is not an option. We could be even more literal and say, *It was an absolute waste of time to...* If we catch ourselves using one of these terms that leaves no wiggle room, we need to back up a bit and examine what's really going on. We need to get honest with ourselves.

If someone is *always* against us, what have we tried to change the situation? And does it actually matter? We often give too much weight to our excuses, circumstances, and people when judging the influence they actually have in our lives. Take the time to evaluate these factors when making decisions to get a clear understanding of how much weight their opinion actually holds. It's likely not as much as we think. If they do truly have enough power over the situation to influence your success, then you need to figure out how to overcome it! There is *always* an opportunity to mend a broken bridge. It's *never* so bad that you're at a point of no return. (Absolutes can hold positive meaning too!) Even if we're telling ourselves that something was an *absolute waste of time*, I can almost guarantee there is a lesson in there somewhere.

Here is a small exercise to help give you some perspective when you feel defeated by something that seems like it was not worth your time or didn't give you the results you were hoping for.

Finish   this   sentence,   *At   least*   _____

_____.

I promise that there was one good thing that came from it. If you can't fill in the blank right now because you truly can't find any good, give it some time. There is likely a silver lining that hasn't come to fruition yet.

It took me a long time to understand the lesson that I was to learn from my high school and college years. I couldn't see that I was the only one who had the power to change any of the situations that I was in. I was taking initiative to change my environment, but because I wasn't changing the way I was approaching it (life), the circumstances appeared to be the same. This gave the illusion that it wasn't my problem; it was just my luck or lack of it. Ultimately, I came to see that the problem was that I wasn't changing anything in myself that would naturally cause a change in my situation. Humans are creatures of habit that like to stay comfortable. Sometimes, true change requires a bit of stretching because the comfort zone is rarely as comfortable as it first appears. It feels comfortable as we are living from day to day, but one day in the future, we'll wake up and wish that we had pushed ourselves harder toward the reality we wanted. We will realize that we have been the barrier to our own success.

Leading from Fear

I didn't want to waitress anymore, although I do truly believe that every person should have to be a server at least once. There is nothing more humbling than knowing your entire livelihood is based on your effort to be kind to people (and have the ability to multitask). I went searching for a job online to see what I could find. If nothing else, whatever I ended up doing would help me to get some of the experience that I was apparently lacking.

There was a job opportunity for an administrative assistant to the director of nursing at a dementia facility. I missed the healthcare industry after having taken a break for a few years, plus this field held a level of comfort I had been missing. But I had only ever been on the direct-care side. I had always wanted to be on the administrative side of healthcare, something I watched my mom excel at my whole life. Maybe I would even get to use my degree that, up until this point, had only been used as an *excuse* to be bitter.

I got an interview and left the building thinking I had nailed it. I would absolutely get the assistant position.

Instead, they called me two days later with an offer to become the new housing manager for the building, which meant I would be overseeing all of the activities, housekeeping, and maintenance staff, as well as working alongside the director of nursing to manage the medical staff.

What?

Silver Lining.

It only took me a few months in my new leadership position to realize that I had absolutely no idea what I was doing. The only experience I had managing people was ... none. I went to school for management, but it was all supply chain, finance, and marketing. Apparently, I had not done a great job with my class lineup because it didn't support this kind of position. I would walk into what we called a *neighborhood*, and immediately start scanning the room for what was wrong that I should fix. I would look for people who seemed out of place—not doing what *I thought* they should be doing—and tell them what they were doing wrong. I made assumptions based on what I thought should be the main priority for the staff and then assumed I was right without any further investigation or thought. Want to take a guess at how popular I was with the employees? I fired multiple people, and even more people quit. (Not always because of me, but I'm sure I didn't help.)

Despite those shortcomings, I was amazing with the tenants and their families. Serving people has always been my strong suit. But when it came to working with the staff, I don't think I even knew I had a problem. I thought I was doing what a manager was *supposed* to do. I was managing. I can now say with certainty that I know exactly why I acted and led the way that I did. I was scared. I was leading with fear as my main driver. I was scared they would find out I was a fraud. I had no experience, and most of the time, I didn't know what I was doing. Most of the people I was managing were older than me and had been doing their jobs longer than I had been alive. I was insecure thinking that people were talking about how bad I was at my job. I felt unworthy to be in a job I didn't even technically apply for because, let's be honest, I wouldn't even have tried for this position. (Statistics reveal that women don't apply for jobs unless they are 100 percent qualified.)[13] I was still in my perfectionism mentality; I wasn't willing to give weight to their concerns because I felt that, in order to stay in control, the ideas and decisions had to be mine. Despite not having any confidence in myself, I still showed up with a forced confidence because I thought

---

[13] https://hbr.org/2014/08/why-women-dont-apply-for-jobs-unless-theyre-100-qualified

that's what a boss was supposed to do. I wouldn't let them see me sweat.

Looking back over this journey a few years down the road, it's hard to recall what I was thinking in the moment. I hadn't developed my personal leadership skills enough to even ask myself why I felt so insecure and unworthy to be there. I've learned since that we are often our own worst critics and the last to believe that we actually deserve something we've been given. Regardless of your viewpoint on faith, if you are put in a position you don't feel ready for, sometimes you need to reach for some faith and believe that you were put there for a reason. It takes a certain level of emotional intelligence to have this conversation with yourself. I was not there yet.

One year into my position as manager, my husband and I welcomed our daughter into the world. Four months later, COVID-19 changed everything I thought I knew. I realized very quickly that I was in over my head in my job. I didn't know how to handle the emotions of telling family members that they couldn't see their loved ones other than through a window. All of the tenants in our memory care facility had some form of dementia, so they did not understand why their sons and daughters couldn't come in. They couldn't understand why their grandkids were showing them their new great-grandbabies through a window instead of getting to hold them. When new tenants would move in, our staff would move the furniture and bring all of their personal belongings into their new room and set it up, rather than their family members. Can you imagine saying goodbye to your parent at the door and not being able to help them get settled into their new home?

As the housing manager, a lot of the blame for this situation was put on my shoulders. I could have projected the blame onto someone else, but it wouldn't have been helpful for me to say, *I am being given instructions from the director of nursing who is getting those instructions from multiple phone calls each day from the higher ups.* Our hands were tied, and all we could do was take responsibility for the hurt, do our best to make things better, and keep moving forward. I was learning to take responsibility and shift away from letting fear lead.

The Change Maker

Six months after my daughter was born, and two months after COVID-19 restrictions were put into place, I decided I needed to take control of something that I actually had a say in: my weight. I had not lost any weight after having a baby. Between the time commitment of my job, and switching off parenting roles with my stay-at-home husband (who was still working himself), I was not taking care of my physical or mental health. A lack of childcare during the pandemic meant that, as soon as I got home from work, I took over the parenting so my husband could do his work. It was so easy to use COVID-19 and the circumstances placed on the world, as an excuse not to take responsibility for my own frustration—everyone was in a state of shock and overwhelm. I had been perfectly fine to join the rest of the world in waiting to see what would happen. But at some point, something had to give. I didn't want to wait anymore.

I had been following someone online for a while, watching from a distance as she lost weight quickly after her second baby. She seemed to be bright and bushy-tailed all of the time! I know that social media has a way of showing us people's highlight reels, but either way, I wanted the energy and optimism she had. I reached out to her to ask what she was doing to lose weight. She informed me that she was a Beachbody coach, and it was her job to help people hold themselves accountable for exercising and eating healthier. Her specific superpower was helping new moms find joy in exercise and their bodies again. Sign me up! I was ready to stop sitting on the sidelines of my own life.

She hosted a 5:30 a.m. virtual accountability group, where women would come together to hold one another accountable to their goals. During the first week of attending these calls, she said something that would forever change my life.

"The difference between someone who will be successful in their attempts to lose weight and change their eating habits, and someone who won't, is personal development."[14]

Later, I would discover that weight loss was my path to learn what personal development had to offer. Saying that we are going to change our lives is too broad. We need something smaller and more definable to learn the lessons that one day could have the power to change our lives. Others may choose to apply personal development to their career, faith, or being a good parent or friend. Our paths will all look different, but I can tell you one thing I now know to be true, (and I'll say it again for those in the back) *The difference between someone who will be successful in their attempts at any goal and someone who won't, is personal development.*

I started with the book *Finish: Give Yourself the Gift of Done*, by Jon Acuff. It is still one of my all-time favorite personal development books. I remember the shift from feeling like I *had* to work out, to being excited that I *got* to work out. I loved the feeling of waking up at 4:30 a.m. to feed my daughter, and then feeling excited that I got to go downstairs to read and workout while it felt like the rest of the world was still asleep.

I had been working out since I was in high school, so that part wasn't out of the ordinary, but what was different was the fact that I was on the last day of a six week program. I had never been able to stick with something for that long! The content of the book I was reading was pushing me to *finish* what I had started. But on the last

---

[14] Katy Fassett, https://www.instagram.com/katy.fassett/

day of the program, the normal 20-minute exercise video I was expecting didn't stop at the 20-minute mark. The video was still going at 30 minutes. Then 35 minutes. I stopped the workout to see how much time was left, and there was still 25 minutes to go ... I threw up my hands, said I was satisfied with the 35 minutes, (it was already longer than I would typically go anyway) and I sat down on the couch to start taking off my shoes. I looked over at this book sitting next to me and had an internal debate about my next steps (I do this *a lot*!). I could be done with the workout—technically, I did what I had shown up to do—20 minutes was plenty. But with the book sitting next to me, I knew I wouldn't be able to say I had completed the program if I didn't *finish* the last 25 minutes. I tied my shoes, got off the couch, and finished.

Everything changed after that, one book at a time. I saw the power that reading and engaging in personal development could have. My mindset improved because of the books I was reading (and the podcasts I was listening to), everything from books about how to set goals, how to be happier, how to be a better leader, and how to build better relationships. I started to lose weight and become more confident in my physical appearance. I became more engaged at home because I was excited to go on walks, play with my daughter, have dance parties, and cook healthy meals. I began to communicate better at work because I started to understand what it looked like to be empathetic to a situation even if I didn't truly understand it. I started to ask the employees their opinions instead of trying to fix problems by myself. I would ask people how they thought It would best be handled. Did they want me to address the person they were having a problem with or did they just need to vent? Most of the time, people are upset in the moment and just need an opportunity to talk it out to begin to see some perspective. In hindsight, I realized I had been robbing people of the opportunity to take responsibility and rectify the problem on their own because I always assumed that they wanted me to just fix the issue.

By following my coach's example, I began to understand what it meant to be the optimistic person in other people's lives. I wanted my positivity to be contagious to those I was leading. I wasn't pretending or following the *Fake it till you make it* philosophy either, I was truly more optimistic. I was coming into my confidence as a leader. John Maxwell co-wrote a song (feat. Bobby Hamrick) that, after several years of working through my personal development journey, brought me to tears the first time I heard it ... and every time since then.

"Gotta find myself, to know myself, to be myself, to improve myself, to get over myself so I can give myself to you."[15]

It's the exact journey I was going through, and it all came down to getting out of my own way, out of my own head, and getting over my need to be right, so I could truly start adding value to those I was leading.

I started to push back in my employees' defense when it came to rules and regulations I didn't understand in regards to COVID-19. I found confidence in my ability to step out of my comfort zone and have hard conversations with understanding and empathy. I often asked people if they needed a hug. It was still frowned upon at this point because of COVID-19, but sometimes, it's just what people need. Especially after a year (plus) of living with very limited physical contact. I can't even tell you how many people took me up on my offer. To this day, offering a hug is still one of my go-to conflict resolution tools. If nothing else, it gets people to chuckle at the awkwardness of the thought!

I read once that a definition of loyalty is staying until the job is done or the project is finished. I always make the joke that COVID-19 broke me because it coincided with when I left the company. But

---

[15] https://www.pandora.com/artist/john-c-maxwell/get-over-myself-feat-bobby-hamrick/ALdppjVhZJn4ttK

in all reality, COVID-19 *broke* me out of my shell. I realized that I wanted to do more and have more of a presence in a place that could inspire real change in its people. I had been in healthcare a long time and it had always felt safe. But I no longer felt the insecurities that made me want to stay in my comfort zone. I was ready to get really uncomfortable and continue climbing my way to leading with confidence.

I left the dementia facility on good terms with everyone. My staff (who at one point was likely scared of me) gave me a gift, hugged me goodbye, and wanted pictures of us as a group to commemorate our time together. I still have the gift because it will remain a symbol of how much I had changed in such a short amount of time. They will forever be the team that stuck by my side while I did a lot of growing up. And I will forever be thankful for the grace and understanding they showed me during that process.

Love, Loss, and Leadership

I wanted to be the typical things kids dream of growing up. I would always play the teacher to my sister's student. I danced in our living room, making up silly dances with my cousins that we would present to our parents. At one point, I wanted to be an author and even wrote and illustrated my own book (funny how we eventually come full circle!). But from the time I was ten, I fully understood what I wanted to be—I wanted to be just like my mom. She worked in healthcare administration, and I admired her from a very young age as she brought me with her on the weekends so she could finish up her work. I watched as she headed one of the committees that worked to build a new hospital. I watched as she spread papers around her at night when she had to bring her work home. I watched as she took days off and still needed to be near a phone in case anyone needed her. Even from a young age, I admired her dedication.

She loved her job. She told us often how happy it made her. My mom and I had people-pleasing in common. We wanted to be everything to everyone—indispensable to the people we encountered. We wanted to have the answers to any question that could be asked, and if we didn't know, we were willing to do what it took to find them (all first-born, over-achieving perfectionists are nodding in agreement right now). Several years later, whenever I run into someone who knew my mom from her work, they tell me how much they loved her, how she always had a smile on her face, and was kind to everyone.

My husband says I have a "phone voice" as my tone changes when I answer the phone, appearing a lot happier than I was prior to answering it. My mom did the exact same thing. When I am missing my mom, I find a video of a still frame photo of her at work in full scrubs after delivering something to the surgery department. The audio behind the photo is her outgoing work voicemail message. She sounded so happy as she called herself the materials manager. She loved her job, and I will never take that for granted.

I wanted to be like my mom. I wanted to be in healthcare administration. It's why I put in so many years of direct care. Nursing school was never an option because chemistry and biology were almost the death of me in college, but business classes I could do (although, statistics and accounting took a stab at trying to kill me, as well). I ended up managing a healthcare facility, so I'd say I completed my childhood dream. This isn't a story of a kid pursuing a career because her parent wanted to live vicariously through her; it is one of absolute admiration for a woman who was a wonderful mom and loved her job with everything that she had.

But, that was just the surface of my mom's story and her influence on me. After leaving healthcare in search of somewhere I could really test myself (and continuing to read all of the books I could get my hands on) I noticed many of the ways my mom managed and led her department were not what the *experts* would recommend now.

To describe my mom as *just* my mom would do a disservice to the relationship that we had. My mom was my best friend, my role model, the grandma to my babies, and the hardest-working and kindest person you would ever meet.

I got a call from my dad 24 hours after we brought my son home from the NICU. My mom had been at work when she looked down at the phone in her hand and realized she couldn't actually feel it. Thankfully, she worked in a hospital and started to walk herself to the ER. Someone offered her a wheelchair halfway down the long corridor and ran her the rest of the way. That night, I packed up my four-week-old son, and my two-and-a-half-year-old daughter, and drove three hours to the hospital she was flown to after determining she had suffered a stroke. My husband dropped my son and me off at the hospital doors, and we walked through the maze of elevators and floors until we finally found her room in the ICU. They wouldn't let me come back the next day. My son was too young, he wasn't allowed to be in the ICU where there were still a lot of people infected with severe cases of COVID. Because of restrictions that said only two people could visit her during the course of her stay, that night was one of only three times I got to see my mom before she passed away two months later from a second stroke.

The story of those 60 days is hard for me to remember, mostly from newborn sleep deprivation but also because so much of that time was spent in a state of unknown. Something I remember very clearly is driving to her workplace with my dad to clean out her office. The job that meant everything to her was now going to be turned over to someone else.

After she passed, I heard multiple people attribute her death to stress from her job. That's not fair to her workplace or the people who work there. I also overheard someone say that my son being in the NICU was a big reason for the stress she had been under. That's not fair either. Blaming others, especially in our pain, is common and comes from fear. But, I want to share my mom's story and bring awareness to the role fear plays in our work lives. Making decisions out of fear is destructive, and I had just begun to share the leadership skills I was learning with my mom.

I spent a lot of time questioning whether or not I should share this piece of my mom's story because it's her story to tell, and she's not here for me to ask her permission. Because of this, I need you to know that what I'm about to tell you, I do not take lightly.

Throughout the 31 years my mom worked at the hospital, she saw employees promoted, leave/quit, and be fired, seemingly for no good reason and having no idea it was going to happen. As you can imagine, this would make anyone who was left question their job security. We know that there are two sides to every story, and in the case of those who get fired, there are more than two. There are the employees that get fired, there's the boss who fires them, and there are all of the bystanders who question what just happened.

Every part of my mom's story is relatable; she operated in her work the way so many of us do. It's common to work late, sometimes taking our work home whether it's because we're scared to be reprimanded for not finishing our tasks, or we want to feel needed. We struggle to delegate our work. Sometimes because we fear losing control of something we will be held responsible for, sometimes because we lack trust in those we are delegating to. Sometimes we just want to remain more knowledgeable than those who are working around us. We are careful not to hire overqualified people, because we don't want them to overshadow us and the work we've already painstakingly done. We don't want to feel replaceable. If you've seen employees fired for what seems like no good reason, it creates fear that you will be next, making you feel even more on edge about letting someone in on the inner workings of your every day.

We do these things, and feel this way, because we are leading with fear—fear of losing something that means so much to us. Fear of becoming insignificant. Fear of not being needed. Fear of losing financial stability that we worked hard for. Even when we know that we aren't leading the way the *experts* recommend, we often feel that it's too late to change, or that we wouldn't know where to start if we could.

I have heard countless stories of children who have lost a parent, seemingly due to stress of a job. I understand that it's incredibly easy to blame their deaths on their work. Hearing my mom's story, and other similar situations, without any understanding of the main character's backstory, it's easy to come to the same conclusion. If I attempted to look at my mom's story from the lens of someone who didn't know her, I would view it the same way.

I could see myself blaming their bosses who seemingly created a culture of mistrust by letting people go (even though we have no understanding of the situation). I can see myself blaming their employees for being late, not taking responsibility and accountability for their work, and then their bosses take on even more stress. I can see myself blaming HR for not taking more disciplinary action toward coworkers that don't take on their load of the tasks. There are endless numbers of people to blame if you are an outsider looking in on a situation without all the information.

Because I'm not an outsider, and I watched my mom's story unfold throughout my life, I can tell you that my mom put herself in this situation. She knew what she was doing and understood the consequences of it. She knew that she was the only one who could change the trajectory of her problems. Most people likely wouldn't understand why she had to work until 7 p.m. and then still go to work on the weekends. My mom and I talked about making the choice to stay late and go in early. She was making the choice to take on the majority of the workload by herself and not delegate. She was making the choice of who to hire and avoiding who to fire. All of these choices were made because she loved her job. To her, the choice was as simple as that.

I remember a conversation I had with her as we were walking into the NICU when she came to spend a day with me and my son just a few days before she had her first stroke. I told her that all of the leadership books say you should hire people smarter than you in certain areas. Being a leader is not about being able to do all of the work, but to hire and inspire people who have strengths in your areas of weakness. It wasn't about making yourself indispensable by doing all of the work, but by making yourself indispensable by growing leaders. Setting boundaries and allowing employees to use their strengths and passions to get the job done are important aspects of good leadership, while also allowing room to ask questions and make mistakes. She said she wasn't sure how she was going to go about making some changes, but she knew she had to try.

Coming from me, it felt a bit like the pot calling the kettle black. I hadn't shared with her all of my experiences in leadership those first few years, mostly because I was embarrassed, but a lot of the frustration she was feeling was all too familiar to me. I wanted so badly to show her the light, and help her lift the weight off her shoulders by applying the tools I was learning.

This story is one of so much love: the love I have for my mom, the love she had for me, and the love she had for her job. But this story is also about fear. Loving something so much that you are scared to lose it. Always grasping at straws, praying that the combination of your decisions will result in stability that chases away the fear—fear of being unworthy of the position you hold, and having someone figure out you don't deserve to be there are horrible feelings to manage.

Leading from love and fear have a lot of the same qualities. Regardless of which space you lead from, you may still be missing one key ingredient: *self*. Putting ourselves at the center of our problems and taking responsibility for our solutions can change the trajectory of our lives. We must build our self-engagement, self-worth, and self-awareness, creating a strong foundation of self.

CHAPTER 4: BUILDING A FOUNDATION OF SELF

"God's gift to you is more talent and ability than you could possibly use in your lifetime. Your gift to God is to develop as much of that talent and ability as you can in a lifetime."[16]
- Steve Bow

I felt really proud of the way that I handled my son being in the NICU. My husband and I were able to play to one another's strengths in handling the situation with as much grace as we could manage. I was proud of the fact that I was able to keep so many of my habits in place while dealing with a hard situation. But when my mom had her first stroke, I anticipated having it all crumble. I felt surprised that a lot of my habits were still holding strong even during the most difficult time in my life. I still wanted to work out—my body had become accustomed to it—even throughout my pregnancy. I still wanted to read books and listen to podcasts. Some would say that it's a crutch to constantly listen to someone else's content rather than allowing silence, so you can listen to your own thoughts ... and in those moments I was OK with that. It would have been easy to push people away and say I just wanted to be alone, and sometimes I did. But I had friends who came to spend

---

[16]https://www.lib.sfu.ca/help/cite-write/citation-style-guides/chicago/secondary-sources#:~:text=The%20style%20manual%20discourages%20writers%20from%20citing%20secondary,of%20the%20secondary%20work%2C%20ot he%20source%20you%20consulted.

time with me, sometimes full days when I was on maternity leave. They knew I needed them, even if I couldn't admit it. I am proud that I was able to keep these practices in place, but I often remind myself that it took over two years of consistency to build that foundation.

Recently, I was pushing my son in his stroller and watching my daughter bike without training wheels in front of us. I was brought back to a moment in time a few years earlier when I was pushing my daughter on the same path. She was six months old, and I was feeling pretty hopeless. I had just begun my weight loss and personal development journey, and I had such a long way to go to get to where I wanted to be at that time. I was constantly being pulled between wanting to be healthy, wanting to have great friends, wanting to love my career, and feeling like it was all just too hard. I felt further than I wanted to be from where I was. But as I came back to the present moment, it hit me. I will never truly be back in that place of helplessness. I will never have to go back to the very beginning. Every lesson I've learned along the way and the mistakes I had to overcome are now lessons I get to take with me in everything that I do. I know what it looks like to build upon a foundation of not only your strengths, but also your weaknesses, and to continuously build a stable, strong, and engaging life—a life you love and that you get to *choose*!

It wasn't enough to feel like I had figured it out, I wanted to help others. Not only those who were in a place of helplessness but those who were just complacent and knew there was more. So, I decided to deconstruct the life I had built and examined the pieces that helped me build this life that I love. The Foundation of Self Framework is the result of that work. It is built on four separate ideas, all of which combine to help you construct a strong and stable foundation for your life. The framework provides you with something to build upon as you continue to learn more about yourself and what would truly make you happy.

Throughout the next few chapters, I will break down the different tiers in the Foundation of Self Framework, what they mean, and specific ideas as to how you can use them in your life. For a quick overview (so you know what you're getting yourself into), go to desireepetrich.com/foundation.

Tier One is Self-Engagement

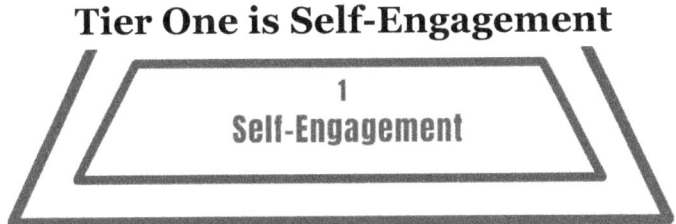

The first tier in the Foundation of Self Framework is *self-engagement*. This first tier is made up of all of the habits and daily disciplines that we have control over in some form or another. I understand that there are always exceptions, and some things are truly out of our control, but several categories make up this tier for a reason. Everyone needs to start somewhere, and that starting point is different for everyone.

Your Foundation of Self is strengthened by the amount of time and effort you put into each of the core habits and values that make up your life. I have 12 categories that I have focused on over the course of the time I have been intentionally working toward personal growth. The 12 categories are physical health, mental health, relationships, personal development, hobbies, environment, sleep, career/skills, faith, boundaries, courage, and money mindset. You can't be amazing at all of these things at the same time; there are not enough hours in a day. However, you can continuously work to improve your discipline and consistency in each of these areas. So let's break them down.

Before I begin this list, please understand that I have described what these categories mean to me, and it is going to look different for you. Physical health to you might mean cold plunges every morning, drinking pressed juice every day, and choosing veganism because it's healthier for you. Um ... no thank you! (Besides, my husband has already said he'll leave me if I ever give up dairy or meat *voluntarily*). My list is based on the things that I do to find balance and feel good about my Foundation of Self. This is not an exhaustive list, but I hope it gives you a good idea of the things I have incorporated into my life to ensure I am building a strong foundation.

Physical Health

What does physical health mean to you? Do you typically refer to metabolic health (blood pressure, pulse, etc.?) Body composition? Musculature, cardiovascular endurance, flexibility, balance, sexual health, tobacco and alcohol consumption? The list could go on and on.

For me, physical health includes 10,000 steps a day (less for the physical benefits and more for the mental motivation to move). I aim to stretch at least ten minutes every night so I can sleep more soundly. I try to have the best posture I can throughout the day. I really struggle with this one. (I sat up straighter as I reread that sentence!) Physical health, to me, includes taking supplements recommended to me by my chiropractor. I *attempt* to eat healthy (I've tried to convince myself that I don't like things like Pop-Tarts and donuts, so I'm not so tempted to include them in my daily foods—it only works some of the time). You will notice that I use the words *aim, try, attempt,* etc. They all seem to be non-committal words, but to pretend I was flawless in my pursuit of my physical health would be a disservice to you. The most we can do is everything that we can do, and that doesn't ever translate to being perfect.

When I was 16, my cousin and best friend, who was six years older than me, was married to a strongman. This doesn't just mean that he was a *strong man*; he competed in strongman competitions in which competitors are tested for their pure strength using a variety of tests, such as the log press, truck pull, Atlas stones, and The Yoke.[17] I fell in love with watching the men and women in these competitions where they were ultimately competing against themselves and their own limitations. I knew that I wanted to be someone who could push the limits of my own abilities.

I have enjoyed exercise and strength training ever since. I take pride in being strong and never backing down when it comes to a challenge. One of my favorite things about exercise is that I get to use all of the lessons I have learned from personal development books and podcasts. I have to coach myself through hard moments from not wanting to start the workout, all the way through the hardest moments where I could easily quit. I am competing with no one other than myself, and I have to hold myself accountable to finish the workout and give it everything I've got.

My second favorite thing about exercise is that my efforts and opinions are ever evolving. At one point, I had convinced myself I hated yoga; it felt too slow. But when I was pregnant with my daughter, I had to slow down on some of the more intense physical activities, and I had an opportunity to fall in love with yoga— something that I never thought I would say. This just goes to show that we all have preconceived notions about the things that we do or do not like. We have to try to make a habit of reserving judgment about something until we've given it a fair shot!

Water intake is a huge part of physical health, and this is one area my family doesn't struggle with. For this book, I went around

---

[17]
https://www.topendsports.com/sport/list/strongman.htm#google_vignette

and counted all of the water bottles we have in our home. We have (2)112 oz., (3) 64 oz., (5) 32 oz., (2) 28 oz., and I stopped counting my kids' water bottles after ten. I have been a big water drinker for as long as I can remember, but I truly don't recall when I started and how it became a habit. It may have been because I was trying to distract myself from not eating out of boredom. It could have been because at some point someone explained the benefits of hydration to me. The fact that I don't remember just illustrates that the path of least resistance is going to be different for everyone. Find what works for you, and once you've made it a habit, *don't stop*!

Newton's first law of motion states that an object at rest remains at rest.[18] The greatest amount of effort needs to be applied to start the motion. Great discipline is needed to get started. Even before we see progress, we need to keep pushing through. As we start to see some movement in the right direction, there will likely be less resistance, but that's because an *object in motion* (a habit, in our case) *stays in motion*. Once we stop, it's going to take just as much effort, if not more, to get the action started again. We get to use our new—and hard earned—results as a motivation to follow through on our goals, remembering how good it feels to accomplish something we set out to do!

Relationships

One day, I received a text from my cousin. It was a link to a TikTok video and below it she wrote, "This made me think of you." As I began to watch the video, I questioned if she sent me the wrong video. It was about how Walt Disney designed the trash-can system at Disney World. I continued to watch, because, although I couldn't figure out what about this video made her think of me, the story was still interesting.

---

[18] https://www1.grc.nasa.gov/beginners-guide-to-aeronautics/newtons-laws-of-motion/

The creator of the video went on to say that Walt Disney was extremely selective about where he put the trash cans around Disney World. He realized that the cleaner a place is, the more likely an individual will make an effort to keep it clean. He did some research about how far an individual would walk to put something into the trash before just throwing it on the ground. The magic number was 30 feet. So, very intentionally, he put a garbage can every 30 feet throughout the entire park. They were also painted to match the theme of the park they were in. There is also a rumor that there is an underground trash system so no "custodial cast member" will have to actually empty the trash. I have done some additional research on this, and that last piece is partially accurate.[19]

As I neared the two-minute mark in the video, I still couldn't understand why she would send this to me, or why it made her think of me? But then the message changed. The woman started talking about how Walt Disney's attention to detail with the trash cans reminds her what it means to be intentional about relationships. In our relationships with our friends, family, and colleagues, we often overlook the opportunities where we could make something easier for someone else. It's so easy to celebrate big things like anniversaries and birthdays. Usually, that highlight reel is posted to social media, and all we have to do is add our comment to the hundreds of other comments that day, and we feel like we made a meaningful connection. But what about the random Tuesday? "There is nothing like a *Love you* or a *Thinking of you* text on a dreary Wednesday." She finished with the question, "What are the garbage cans of your life? And how can you make it better

---

[19]https://www.wdwinfo.com/disney-merchandise/the-art-of-disneys-trash-cans/#:~:text=The%20Basic%20Design%20and%20Walt's%20Impact&text=He%20found%20that%2030%20feet,Frontierland%20alone%20has%20over%20120!

and more intentional?" (I could not find the original video. I think it was taken down, so this is based on my memory of the video.)

It finally clicked why she would send this to me. I am also someone who sends a lot of dreary Wednesday afternoon texts. A random, *I was thinking about you today, and I wanted you to know that I miss you!* Or, I follow up about a conversation I had with someone recently just to check in and let that person know I had been thinking about her or him. I believe there is a reason why people pop into your thoughts at random times. I try to use those opportunities to ask someone out to lunch or schedule a playdate with our kids. Sometimes, I'll send five dollars over Venmo to a friend to get a cup of coffee if I know that person has had a tough week.

I also rarely write on people's Facebook pages for their birthdays or comment "happy anniversary" on a Facebook post. I do however appreciate social media for the reminder of these big occasions. If I see that it's someone's birthday or anniversary, and I know that person well enough to feel it would mean something for me to reach out, I text them or call them. I don't ever expect a response in return, but I hope that it makes them smile. If it's someone I don't know well enough to text them or send a separate message, I make a mental note that it's that person's birthday. I can't tell you how many times I have run into an acquaintance at the grocery store, and I've been able to say "happy anniversary" or "happy birthday" to someone even though we've only met a few times. The amount of connection this creates is like no other, and it takes me less than a minute to check the birthdays in the morning.

I don't say these things to brag. I still have to remind myself to ask people how they're doing when we're in person after I've just finished updating them about my life. It's not that I don't care—I do—I'm just always in my head, thinking about lots of other things.

So, it is not a simple thing for me to ask about others. That's why I am intentional about reaching out to people when I think of them.

So, let me turn this around and pose this question to you: *What are the Disney trash cans in your life? What could you be more intentional and purposeful about in your life to create deeper relationships?*

Personal Development

I want to ask you an important question: *What's the difference between personal development and personal growth?*

Lucky for you, I have the answer!

I define personal development as the intentional act of learning ways to strengthen our Foundation of Self. It's listening to podcasts, reading books, and listening to audio books. It's having conversations with people outside of our comfort zone and working to understand more than our own point of view. Personal development is the act of setting goals and working toward them every day. It's the intentional work that we put behind what we say we want. For me, a large part of personal development has been getting out into my community, joining ambassador programs and boards, attending charity events, and meeting new people.

Personal growth is something that we earn along the way. I think of it as every time we take a risk and get out of our comfort zone, we're either going to be successful, or we're going to learn something. Failure is the backbone of personal growth. It's how we learn lessons about what works and what doesn't. It's how we grow stronger, even in really hard and what sometimes seem like impossible moments. We become more confident because when we put in the work, over and over again, we prove to ourselves that we follow through on what we say we're going to do.

Personal growth is knowing that in order to reach the top of the hill, we have to climb over our failures and use our mistakes as stepping stones of what *not* to do. We get to use the relationships that we've built to help us climb higher and maybe even take someone with us. It's the gold star we earn every time we put intentional action toward our development. The *growth* part is what everyone wants right? In order to get it, you need to put in the work and the time to develop it.

Hobbies

Take a moment to list your hobbies. Did you make it past one? Two?

I rarely work with a coaching client that can name more than one hobby. Some think that it would be selfish to take time away from their responsibilities, like their job, spouse, or children. Others don't know what kind of hobby they want to have, so they're stuck in no-man's land, wishing they had something more productive than TV and social media to fill their time. Some have a spouse that has enough hobbies for the both of them, and they don't feel they have the time, all things considered.

I'm here to tell you that the definition of a hobby is whatever you want it to be! My hobbies are exercise and reading. Based on that information, I realize there's a chance you've now decided to discount what I have to say, because, well, I must be crazy! But hear me out.

I have conditioned myself to love these things, slightly out of necessity. I began by trying to read every single Nora Roberts book I could get my hands on. (I only made it through three quarters of her 200+ books.) From there, I started to branch out into other romance novels, then other fiction books, and finally, I started to read some personal development books. (I was 25 before I ever made it through a nonfiction book.)

Like books, I conditioned myself to love exercise. And don't think that means I don't have to convince myself to participate every once in a while (OK, most of the time). The things that we know are good for us, and even the things that we enjoy, are sometimes the things we have the hardest time following through with. Don't get me wrong, exercise is still a chore. It's something I check off of my to-do list every day. But it's also an activity that helped me build a community of friends, and it's something that allows me to set boundaries by choosing exercises I like, rather than being swayed by what social media claims is the new be-all and end-all of exercises.

One time, a client told me that she didn't have time for hobbies because she was too busy working, raising her kids, and volunteering in her community. I'm pretty sure I was smiling internally because I had a feeling I knew how this conversation was going to end. But the magic of personal development does not lie in someone telling you how things are. You aren't going to magically believe them and then apply it to your life. (If that were the case, we'd all be thin, rich, and fearless). It's about asking the right questions and doing the work to come to the conclusions yourself.

I asked her if she liked her job. Her response was, "I love my job." I asked her if she enjoyed volunteering, and she said, "I love volunteering. It's a way I get to spend time with my daughter and give back to my community." As we continued this game of back and forth, you could visually see her thought process begin to change. She was starting to realize she enjoyed the things that she was using as an excuse for why she couldn't have the things that she really wanted. She assumed she didn't have hobbies because her whole life revolved around work and her community. *But that's what she loved!* At the end of our time together, she realized the way she spent her time each week wouldn't change much, but her mindset around what she thought she *had* to do, versus what she *wanted* to do changed. She was able to find more joy in those things, simply because she was looking at them differently.

You can love fishing, hunting, sports, and video games. You can love cooking, knitting, and volunteering. You may even meet some of your best friends while doing these things. You can love things that are going to move the needle forward and help you to become the person that you want to be. The first tier builds on itself. When you put work into any of the categories, other areas will likely improve, as well. How can you build hobbies into your life that will help you strengthen your courage? Your money mindset? Your physical and mental health? I'm glad you asked!

Your Turn!

Although I didn't go through all 12 of the foundational categories I have listed, I went through the ones that originally hit home for me. But if I asked you to look through the 12 pillars, and pick the ones that you wanted to focus on—ones that you thought would be the biggest change-makers for you—they would likely look very different from mine. So, I want to finish up this section by asking a question I'm sure you've had since you started this chapter: How *do I accomplish all, or realistically any, of these things when I have failed over and over to incorporate healthy habits into my life?* Here is my argument to anyone who uses failure as an excuse to not try again, *You still learned something!* Every single time you set a goal for yourself that you don't complete, you learn something about yourself. You learn which parts work and which parts don't.

There is a difference between good intentions and being intentional. When we set a goal to sleep more, eat better, exercise more often, be more patient with our kids, spend more time with our spouse, or develop deeper relationships with our friends, those are *good intentions.* Being intentional requires breaking those things down into more actionable and realistic steps. Because what's realistic for me in my current season of life is going to look different for you in yours.

Focus on your progress, not someone else's position.

I don't typically like when books leave sections to journal or ask you questions at the end of the chapter, mostly because I never do it. It makes me feel guilty because I know I should be more willing to do the exercises that have likely worked for other people. So, I'll leave it up to you. Here is an opportunity to set some intentional action steps for yourself and begin to develop some intentional *self-engagement.* You can write them down here, or somewhere else, but don't take this action step lightly. The directions for this exercise are simple. Write down one very small action step that you can take in each area—one that, if you were able to stay consistent in implementing, would have the potential to set you on a trajectory to all of the things you need to reach your full potential. I'll even do it with you.

Next to each category, I have listed my intentional action that I track for each of these categories. You can add your own.

Physical Health (Do 30 minutes of exercise every day.)

_____

_____

Mental Health (Write down 3 things I'm grateful for every day.)

_____

_____

Desiree Petrich

Relationships (Reach out to at least one friend every week to check in on them.)

_____

_____

Personal Development (Read ten pages of a personal development book every day!)

_____

_____

Hobbies (Read books that help me learn, as well as ones that excite me.)

_____

_____

Environment (Tidy up the house every night, so I wake up to a clean house to start my day—keep in mind we have a little house!)

_____

_____

Sleep (Be in bed by 10 p.m. to get enough sleep to wake up at 5 a.m.)

_____

_____

Career/Skills (Attend as many networking events as possible to maintain and build new relationships in the workspace.)

_____

_____

Faith (Pray with my kids every night before bed.)

_____

_____

Boundaries (Make myself a priority by always putting myself and my family above anyone else's agenda.)

_____

_____

Courage (Do it scared, not unprepared!)

_____

_____

Money Mindset (Buy the tools I need to live my best life now!)

_____

_____

Some of my intentional actions may still seem overreaching, and not very actionable on a daily basis. But some of them are mantras I repeat to myself, and then I use the tools I have to help me follow through on them. For example, in the courage category, _Do it scared, not unprepared!_ is something I have to repeat to myself every day. When I run into a limiting belief that tells me I can't do something, when I know that the conversation I am going to have will be hard, or when I need to send an email that I don't want to send, I repeat the phrase and remind myself that I've done hard things in the past, and I was OK. If I need to go deeper, I think of the worst case scenario and come up with a game plan of how to handle it. That's the _prepared_ part!

For a healthy money mindset, my mantra is, _Buy the tools I need to live my best life now._ It's not very often I save for something. This may be controversial, especially if you are frugal like my husband, but I believe in buying the tools to help you to be successful in building a strong Foundation of Self _now_!

I have purchased a massage gun and a cupping set to use at home when I need it. Cupping therapy is an ancient form of alternative medicine in which you put special cups on your skin for a few minutes to create suction. According to the National Library of Medicine, "It has been claimed that cupping therapy tends to drain excess fluids and toxins, loosen adhesions and revitalize connective tissue, increase blood flow to skin and muscles, stimulate the peripheral nervous system, reduce pain, controls high blood pressure and modulates the immune system."[20] Owning these tools makes me more intentional about taking care of my body because it gives me easy access and saves me money doing it myself rather than going to the chiropractor. I will also point out that having these tools points to how well I know myself. I am an over-buyer, which means at any given moment, you will find 34 rolls of toilet paper and five tubes of toothpaste in our closets. I enjoy purchasing items. Buying new things makes me happy, which is why I have an entire section of my weekly newsletter dedicated to some of my favorite products for life and business. You may be an under-buyer, and the thought of buying something for fun seems either frivolous or wasteful. Knowing who you are and what gives you joy is a big part of building on your Foundation of Self in a way that's going to keep it strong and stable for many years to come!

(To check out some of my favorite products, go to desireepetrich.com/favorites.)

I can't finish this chapter without sharing my absolute favorite time management tool with you. It's not block schedules, tracking your time, timing yourself, or scheduling breaks in your day, and trust me when I say I've tried all of those! One of the only tools I have found to help me accomplish all of the things I want to do in a day is something I call *time chunking*. This means that for

---

[20]https://www.ncbi.nlm.nih.gov/pmc/articles/PMC6435947/#:~:text=It%20h as%20been%20claimed%20that,and%20modulates%20the%20immune% 20system

everything I want to do, I ask myself the question, *What is the minimum amount of time I would need to dedicate to this habit every day to feel like I am making progress?*

You'll notice that a lot of my habits are associated with an amount of time. If my goal is simply to *stretch every night*, it likely wouldn't happen—the goal is too broad—and I wouldn't ever feel like I could check it off my list. My goal is also not to *stretch for 45 minutes every night*, which is a long time, and I guarantee I would fall into the all or nothing mindset of, *If I can't finish the entire 45 minutes, it's not worth doing at all.* Because when we make our options all or nothing, we almost always default to nothing. My goal is to *stretch for ten minutes.* When I asked myself the question, *What is the minimum amount of time needed to see progress,* ten minutes was my answer. I asked myself this question when it came to my daily reading habit, how many steps I would get a day, how many hours of sleep I need, how many minutes I needed to spend on certain areas of my business, and several other categories of the self-engagement tier.

This tool is not just beneficial when trying to set the right goals for yourself. This tool is great for filling the pockets of your time with things that you want, without feeling like you have to schedule it into your day. I've seen it too often in myself, and those I work with, that if we schedule our time to the minute, we end up getting frustrated and discouraged when something throws a wrench into our day, and we have to pivot. This is why blocking off my schedule doesn't work for me. Instead, I only schedule the absolute necessities (such as meetings or events), everything else is on a daily to-do list. It doesn't matter when I get it done during the day, as long as I finish the time I set. This helps me to feel more in control of my time, and allows me to set priorities for the day based on how circumstances unfold. I have found that my daily habits are completed much more frequently if I break up my goals this way.

For example, I had a client who really wanted to read more. She had a goal of reading for an hour every night. That may be doable if you have no kids, no house to clean, and no responsibilities after you're off of work for the day. She did not fit into any of those categories! I started to ask some questions to figure out where her roadblocks were, and how we could begin to set a goal that was more realistic. Specifically, one that didn't leave her feeling guilty for not following through or feeling overwhelmed that she never had any time for herself. I'm sure you can relate that if you leave anything to the end of the night, it's not likely to be done. This is exactly what was happening to her.

I started with these questions: Does *this really matter to you at this time in your life? Would it be easier to just cut this goal out for now?* If she had answered *no*, it would have been as simple as taking this off of her to-do list each day. As we discussed in Chapter 1, sometimes the excuses we use for not ever completing the goals that we set for ourselves are just our mind's way of trying to get us to revisit our priorities. In this situation, that was not the case. She wanted to read; she wanted to learn and grow her knowledge, as well as feel like she was doing something for herself.

So, I then asked the next question, *What is the minimum amount of time that you would need to read to feel like you were successful in this goal and making progress?* Her answer was not an hour as she had originally said, but ten minutes. Already, this goal seemed a lot more doable. I followed up this realization with the question, *Is there a reason why you need to read at home, or would it be possible for you to read at work?* I happened to know that one of her goals as a leader was to lead by example. If that is our intention, it's important that we are showing or telling others that we are doing what we say we're going to do and following through. It's inspirational, but it's also relatable when they can see it happening. She started to read at work for ten minutes a day, with her door open so her coworkers could see that she was being intentional about her growth. She wasn't reading every morning from 8-8:10 a.m. Instead, she was finding a ten-minute pocket in her day when she could fit it in.

This is one of hundreds of time management ideas, but I encourage you to ask yourself the right questions to come up with the habits that are going to help you feel successful like you're making progress toward your goals!

Which category are you going to work on? Which formula is going to work for you? You have to try them to find out! No one else can do these things for you; you have to self-engage with the process. Other people can encourage you, bribe you, and maybe even discipline you, but until you actively engage yourself in these activities (for reasons that matter to you) there will be no long-lasting change. Maybe you can't focus on all 12 areas of the foundation right now, because, as I've said, sometimes there just aren't enough hours in the day. So, where can you focus? Ask yourself some questions. Does getting more sleep at night increase your overall attitude and energy level? Will walking more increase your stamina to play with your kids? Will having a better money mindset allow you to easily fix some problems you have control over?

The formula is different for every person. It's based on understanding yourself and a willingness to make yourself a priority. Just remember—one new habit creates a ripple effect. Focus on your foundation in the areas that feel manageable to you, stay consistent until it becomes a habit, and *don't stop*!

For a more detailed journaling exercise on the Foundation of Self Framework, as well as an opportunity to join me for a workshop on goal setting using this framework, visit desireepetrich.com/framework.

CHAPTER 5: REDEFINING SUCCESS

"If at first you don't succeed, redefine success."[21]
- George Carlin

Do you feel confident? If so, does that make you a confident person? Is your confidence tied to your appearance? Your job title? Your standing in the community? What would happen if tomorrow you broke your leg and could no longer lift weights or run? What if you were laid off unexpectedly? If you lost all of your money, and your standing in the community was put into question, would you still feel confident?

Imagine a line. On one side it says "zero confidence," and on the other side it reads, "100% confident." Somewhere in the middle of this imaginary line is a point where you will *feel* confident. (You can replace confidence with anything you're striving for: honesty, discipline, joy, patience, adventure, consistency, etc.) When we want to be more (<u>fill in with what you want</u>), we tend to believe there will be a magical moment when we will suddenly believe it. Something will happen, and we will finally be able to *believe* we are what we say we are and what we are striving to be. I'm going to let you in on a secret—this point will likely never come on its own.

---

[21] https://quotefancy.com/quote/813301/George-Carlin-If-at-first-you-don-t-succeed-redefine-success

Tier Two is Self-Worth

This second tier is about our *self-worth*. Just like we can't leave it to anyone else to define what success looks like for us, we can't leave it to anyone else to decide we're worthy. Believing that we're worthy comes down to loving ourselves first. We have to believe it because we are the only ones who should be mentally and emotionally involved in the process. We will inevitably bring other people and circumstances into the mix; we're human. But we have to make sure that our own definition of success—and the belief in our own self-worth—are our priorities!

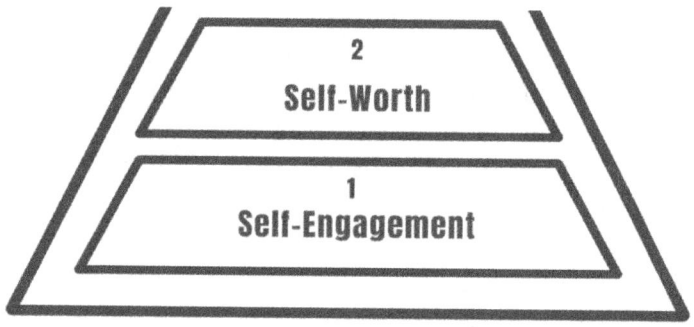

In order to reach this point, we need to put in the work. We need to decide what defines success and what it looks like for us as individuals. When someone labeled me as *disciplined*, I used to feel like an imposter. I may portray discipline to others, but to truly believe it myself was a much harder sell. Only I knew the battles that went on inside my head every time I tried to choose a book over TV or to actually wake up early instead of hitting the snooze button. I have to argue with myself every time I see a cookie. (There is no way I'm disciplined when every decision I make is this hard.)

Eventually, I realized the only way I would be able to feel disciplined was to define what discipline meant to *me*. The technical definition of *discipline* is, "the practice of training people to obey rules or a code of behavior, using punishment to correct disobedience."[22] Harsh. If that was the definition of discipline I was trying to portray, I'd last a day. Instead, I have defined discipline as, *Doing what I say I'm going to do to the best of my ability with the knowledge and information I have at the moment.* We could use this same definition to define *consistency*... and that's the point! We don't have to stick to the textbook definitions; we get to create our own. This way we can include the amount of flexibility in the definition needed in that season of life. For me, it's about putting in the work to ensure I have the tools to make my goals possible. It's about intentionally creating relationships with people who have some of the same goals I do and engaging with those who will push me to follow through, believing in me when I have a hard time believing in myself. The purpose of redefining what we want is not to describe what we already have; it's redefining our goal to personalize it in a way that makes it attainable and exciting!

Jon Acuff wrote an entire book about what it means to guarantee our goals, called *All It Takes Is a Goal: The Three-Step Plan to Ditch Regret and Tap Into Your Massive Potential.*[23] At first, I struggled with the concept because he set goals like *be healthier* and *get better sleep*. This concept was a direct contradiction to what I've always been taught about goal-setting. SMART goals need to be specific, measurable, achievable, relevant, and time-bound.[24] His argument was that if you commit to exercising two days a week, every week for an entire year, you can guarantee that you will be more physically fit than you were the year prior. If your goal is to have a stronger marriage, you can hug and kiss your spouse every day when he or she leaves and returns

---

[22]https://courses.lumenlearning.com/wm-humanresourcesmgmt/chapter/the-purpose-of-discipline/#:~:text=In%20it%27s%20active%20or%20verb,but%20to%20instruct%20and%20correct

[23]https://jonacuff.com/all-it-takes-is-a-goal-book/

[24]https://www.atlassian.com/blog/productivity/how-to-write-smart-goals#:~:text=What%20are%20SMART%20goals%3F,within%20a%20certain%20time%20frame.

home, then sit down at the supper table as a family at least twice a week, and guarantee your marriage will be stronger than it was the year prior.

I went about trying to find my own understanding of what it means to set a goal and complete it. I had reached "success" in a few areas, but how could I deconstruct how I got there to help others who were asking for my advice? The people asking for help didn't have the same goals or dreams that I had. They didn't have the same skills or personality traits as me. They didn't have the same family dynamics, or traumatic experiences. So how could I help them using the same tools that I had used? This is when I developed the second tier of the Foundation of Self. The second tier is about redefining success in a way that makes our goals feel not only attainable but exciting!

Do you want to be more confident, disciplined, honest, joyful, consistent, or authentic? Do you want to have more growth, integrity, adventure, or levity? This list could go on forever, so tailor it to fit your goals and dreams. What do you want more of in life?

In the first tier of the Foundation of Self, the concepts were easy to research. Just ask Google how to improve your mental health and over two billion ideas will populate your page. Ask five friends what their hobbies are, and you've just increased your knowledge of what it means to have a hobby (funny enough, there seem to be those who have too many hobbies to count and those who couldn't name their hobby for a million dollars.) Either way, you'll have a better understanding than when you started.

But how do you help someone who wants to be more confident, more joyful, or more authentic? How do you begin to help someone whose goal is to have more levity in life? What does that even mean?

We can answer these questions in three easy steps: analyze, define/redefine, and follow through.

Analyze

How can you go about analyzing your day? I started with a simple journaling practice of determining how I felt at the end of every day. Was I tired, overwhelmed, excited, or sad? Did I feel like I had been productive or distracted throughout my day? I started to notice a pattern: most days, I felt overwhelmed and unproductive. These feelings were showing up as impatience with my kids and frustration toward my husband. Once I recognized how I was feeling, I started to dig deeper into why I was feeling those things. For example, when I analyzed my day, trying to figure out why I felt so overwhelmed, I realized it was because I was trying to accomplish too much in my day. I was being unrealistic and felt like I couldn't detach from my work when my kids got home from daycare. I was still trying to figure out how I could continue to be productive while my kids wanted to play, supper needed to be cooked, and the house needed to be cleaned. I decided to introduce a little more levity and a bit more playfulness into my evenings. If you're like me and find yourself getting frustrated quickly, you may be able to relate. Just saying that I wanted to be more playful wasn't enough; I needed to define what *being playful* meant to me.

Define and Redefine

How will we know if we've succeeded? How can we be confident that we've incorporated more playfulness, joy, or adventure into our lives if we haven't defined what those things mean for us? During my Foundation of Self workshops, we spend about one-third of the time defining what success means in whatever word we chose. There is something so powerful about hearing five people, who all want to be more consistent, define what *consistency* means to them in five completely different ways.

Desiree Petrich

My definition of playfulness is to *get on the floor*. I know I am a fun mom. I enjoy playing with my kids, but I continuously need to get over the hump of feeling like I have other things I should be doing. I decided to add *play on the floor with the kids for 20 minutes* to my to-do list. I went through the questions I explained for *time chunking* in chapter 4 and decided that 20 minutes is the minimum amount of time I wanted to spend fully engaged with my kids each day. Do I love that I have to add this to my to-do list? No. Is it necessary? Turns out it is. I am not saying that I only ever spend 20 minutes with my kids, but having this listed as a daily goal helps me break the cycle of overwhelm and productivity. Being more playful by getting on the floor (which includes coloring, playing a board game, going outside, throwing a ball, etc.) makes me a better mom and a better person. And if I only get 20 minutes for the day because there truly are other things that need to be done, then I still get to spend some quality time with my kids.

After analyzing my days, I realized I also wanted to stop jumping to anger when something didn't go my way. The question was: What *is the opposite of anger* in this example? My answer was *Levity*. My definition of incorporating more levity was: *Don't allow anger to bubble so quickly. Be able to laugh at things that in the past would have had the ability to break me.* I truly felt like I reached success in this area when I opened my washing machine one night and found there was white fuzz covering every single inch of clothing. I investigated, assuming I had washed a diaper (this would not be the first time!), but I had never seen it get quite that messy. As I was pulling my brand new clothing out of the washer, I found myself growing more and more frustrated that I was now going to have to figure out how to clean my clothing, which is what the washer was supposed to do! I was nearing the bottom of the washer when I pulled out a hard piece of something red, around the size of my fist. It looked familiar. That was when I realized the red piece looked a lot like the book I had just finished reading. It suddenly occurred to me that the practice of putting books in my laundry basket to transport from my bedroom to my desk downstairs was probably not the smartest idea. I burst out laughing! Mostly because it should not have surprised me that this happened. If anything, it should have surprised me that with the hundreds of books I have read over the years, this hadn't happened sooner.

At that moment, I got to celebrate success. It was a situation that in the past would have broken me. I would have jumped to anger and likely tried to blame it on someone else. This was a hard pill to swallow because I was the only one to blame, but on the other side of hard is typically where we find success. I was able to practice levity in that moment. My definition of levity being not allowing anger to bubble so quickly. My immediate reaction was anger, but by remembering that I was working toward levity, I was able to talk myself down. My definition also included being able to laugh at things that in the past would have broken me. Done!

When we define what success looks like, it begins to be less of an unreachable milestone and more like stepping stones of mini celebrations. If we don't take the time to celebrate when we've hit *our* definition of success, then we may need to reevaluate why we want it in the first place or go through the steps to redefine what it looks like at this point in our lives.

What do you want to be more of? If the answer to that question doesn't come immediately to mind, you can borrow from my list: *confidence, discipline, honesty, growth, joy, consistency, productivity, authenticity, integrity, adventure, humor, patience, etc.* Now, take the time to define what success looks like for you. How can you label success in a way that is reachable, not just once, but over and over again?

It takes noticing how we're handling situations and getting better at talking to ourselves through old patterns. Once we begin to experience success more often, we need to consistently celebrate when reaching our goals.

Follow-Through

I want to be more adventurous in life. I set this goal at the old age of 22 after graduating from college (just 30 minutes away from my parents), and I intended to follow through on that goal. When I decided at 24 years old that I was going to marry my college sweetheart, it meant never leaving my college town of around 13,000 people. That number was huge compared to the town of 800 that I grew up in, but I had looked at colleges in different cities and states, so it still felt like a very small number to live with for the rest of my life.

For a long time, I felt like I was neglecting my goal to be more adventurous. I could get my husband to travel with me if we went somewhere close to where our families lived so we wouldn't have to pay for a hotel. That limited us to one destination outside of Minnesota. Honestly, I resented him for this in our early years of marriage. Then I started to go on trips by myself and sometimes with friends; the experiences were never all that I wanted them to be. There were always travel issues. (I once had to sleep on the airport floor after spending three hours on a plane that never left the tarmac.) The trips were expensive, and I still had student loans and a house to pay off. At one point, I decided being adventurous was overrated. But, as I'm sure you can relate, there are societal expectations to want certain things: work-life balance, good physical appearance, friends who make up a community, and an adventurous life where experiences outweigh material goods.

Even though I had decided I was OK with the fact that I'd never left the country and that traveling was not something I desired to do, there was a continuous nagging feeling that I *should* want those things. Because of that feeling, I was in a constant state of guilt that

I wasn't experiencing life like I should. I was sad that I wasn't having *adventures*. I decided to analyze and identify the problem. I realized this feeling wasn't going to go away, and I couldn't just will the feeling out of existence. So instead of feeling guilty for not following through on my goal to be more adventurous, I defined success in this area in a new way. I decided to incorporate adventure in a way that works for me and I could follow through on—I call them mini-adventures.

Every time my family goes to the grocery store together, I call it a mini-adventure. When my best friend and I travel to the sauna studio ten minutes from my house, it's a mini-adventure. When my husband and I take the 30-minute drive to the casino for supper and to spend five dollars on the slot machines (we tried 20 dollars on his birthday once, and ten years later, he still talks about that specific regret!), it's a mini-adventure. Once I analyzed and identified the problem, I was able to redefine what success looks like for me in this area.

If we were to stop after defining what success looks like, we would still experience *failure*. Just because we define what we want doesn't mean it's going to magically manifest our goal into existence. We still need to be intentional about following through and celebrating our success. In fact, our personal development only happens if we are willing to take action. We grow in the process of following through.

When I washed a hardcover book and laughed about it, I labeled it as success. I talked about it with my husband and celebrated in that moment. Every time I get off of the couch at night to do my ten minutes of stretching, I label my discipline as success and celebrate one more day of consistency. Whether celebrating looks like you telling someone about it, crossing it off of a habit tracker, or simply congratulating yourself for following through, those small moments will help build self-confidence and contribute to your overall feelings of self-worth. We may not have to earn it, but that doesn't mean we can't contribute to it!

When we set unrealistic expectations for ourselves, it becomes too hard to imagine that we will ever reach our goal. The gap between where we currently are, and where we want to be, holds too many unknowns and potential breaking points. At the risk of quoting Jon Acuff too often, in one of the earlier podcast episodes on his show, All It Takes is a Goal, he said something along the lines of, *You are not supposed to be able to meet tomorrow's goals with today's skills. You will get bored. Try to find a happy medium between boring and overwhelming, right in the middle is inspiring.*[25]

The best part is that this process does not require perfection. Our ability to react with less anger and more curiosity, humor, or patience will continue to grow over time. Being aware of our desire to change our reactions will make us more quick to course correct when we begin to fall back into old ways. The repetitive practice of catching ourselves with a certain attitude, or having a specific train of thought, will allow us to shift our mindset, until it becomes second nature to react the way we desire.

We could make this exercise easy by defining success in a way that means we've already succeeded, in which case there is nothing left to do. But we would get so bored! We would lose momentum and have no reason to continue working toward anything. We need to find a balance between setting an easily attainable goal (so we feel accomplished) and knowing the *right* goal which will require us to grow to reach it. Going through this process from start to finish provides endless motivation to pull from to keep the momentum going.

---

[25]
https://open.spotify.com/show/4eMV8D1xUxqfSM6VR7kzjT?si=aaf8569
4bc894d5a

CHAPTER 6: WALKING INTO THE WIND

"We need to accept that we won't always make the right decisions, that we'll screw up royally sometimes— understanding that failure is not the opposite of success, it's part of success."[26]
- Arianna Huffington

Every once in a while, I'll go for a walk or a run, and it feels easier than it has in the past, as if all of the time I spent trying to get into better shape is finally paying off and exercise can officially be enjoyable! The excitement is short-lived because when I get to the end of the road and turn back toward home, I realize it felt easy because the wind was at my back, propelling me forward. To add insult to injury, not only had I not progressed as much as I thought, but now I have to go back home *walking into the wind.*

I will never forget a bus ride we took to a track meet when I was in high school. I was a discus and shot put thrower on the track and field team, so what the running coach said didn't directly apply to me, but his words are forever burned in my brain.

It's raining, windy, and overall miserable out there. But this is what you've been training for. The reason we don't let you skip a day of practice when the weather is less than ideal is because you get to practice resistance. You have to

---

[26]https://www.inhersight.com/blog/insight-commentary/quotes-about-failure-will-lift-you-up

run into the wind. You have to run in the rain. You have to endure the cold. But when we're here, at the track meet where it all comes down to moments, you will have a leg up. You will know what it's like to push through. You will be stronger from having fought through the wind and rain, both physically and mentally. So today, when you feel like you can't go any further or faster, put your head down, watch your feet hit the pavement, and remember—you prepared for this very moment.

I paraphrased his words (my memory isn't that good!) but the concept of his speech came back to me one day as I was walking down a gravel road that I had walked hundreds of times. I was walking against the wind on a straight shot from one stop sign to the next. The weather was decent, there were no hills, one set of train tracks, and rarely any vehicles (unless it was farming season). Despite what seemed like a lack of obstacles, the walk felt really hard. I was expending a lot of energy from fighting against the wind. I had to put my head down and swing my arms to cut through the wind. I had to brace my core to avoid getting pushed over, and I had to deliberately put one foot in front of the other. I was determined to get to my destination.

I had walked against the wind many times, but this day felt extra challenging. It felt mentally taxing, and it would have been so easy to give up, to turn around, and be propelled by the wind all of the way back home. That's when the coach's words came back to me, and I knew this is how I'll get a leg up; this is how I will test my physical and mental strength, even when there is nothing on the line. I will begin to train and build trust in myself to know that I will not give up, growing my belief that I can do hard things.

I come back to this pep talk every time I feel like circumstances outside of my control have the ability to stop me in my tracks. I experienced a tragedy that should have broken me—if you had asked me how I would react to losing my mom, I would have told you that I would not be able to function. I would have anticipated a full breakdown. But with a one-month-old son, and my daughter who was just over two, I wasn't able to break down completely. For the two months that my mom was in the hospital recovering from her first stroke, I thought I was continuing to live my life simply because I had no other choice. I had people who were depending on me. I wasn't *allowed* to break down.

It wasn't until six months after she passed that I started to understand—I had been preparing for this event, not intentionally, and not specifically. I still have regrets that haunt me from time to time. I sometimes still feel guilty that I am continuing to live and grow while she's not here. But I began to question how I was able to get through it. My mom was my best friend. It *should* have broken me past a point of no return, but I found myself still feeling joy and excitement. I was still happy and thankful for my life and the family I had.

So why hadn't it broken me completely? Was I masking my depression? Was I still stuck in the denial stage of grief? I've come to understand that I had been walking into the wind for so long (and proving to myself that I could do hard things) that it deepened my faith and strengthened me both physically and mentally. I had built a strong foundation. I had built relationships so strong that my friends traveled hours to be at my mom's funeral. Some of whom had never met her.

I continued to read about personal development throughout the process. I cried when I needed to. I asked for hugs when I needed comfort. I called my friends when I needed support, and I let myself feel the feelings as often as I needed to. I would be lying if I said that following through on these habits every day was easy. My mind was often somewhere else, but because I had built a strong foundation of habits, mindset shifts, and relationships with people who had been there for me, I didn't have to start over from scratch. I didn't have to pick up the pieces by myself.

It would have been so easy to stay in that place of sadness, not only for the situation but sorry for myself that I was put in this position at no fault of my own. Instead, I used the foundation I had built as a way to rise up and out of the hard moments faster than if I had started the process of grief with no support system. The lows didn't last as long because I was strong for having spent so much time walking into the wind.

It wasn't intentional at the time. I developed the Foundation of Self *after* seeing the process of what having a strong foundation looks like. Preparing for hard times to come is not the same thing as having a pessimistic mindset. It's understanding that to be human means things won't always be perfect. Building a strong foundation allows us to prepare for hard times in a way that feels authentic to us as an individual.

It honestly pains me to write this next part. There is a lot of vulnerability in showing my weakest moments, but I truly believe the best lessons can be learned in times of struggle.

Eighteen months after my mom passed away, I was still doing all of the foundational things: reading, exercising, spending time and energy building friendships, praying, journaling, etc. But I felt myself becoming stressed. My body was tired, my mind was on overload, and my relationships with my husband and kids were becoming strained because of my never-ending to-do list for my budding business. But I kept pushing. I wasn't willing to lose the momentum. I wasn't willing to stop. Honestly, I was scared shitless by what it would mean to stop moving. Turns out, there was a reason for that.

I had been attending a gym that I absolutely loved! The coach was amazing, the girls I worked out with were inspiring and some of the strongest women I had ever met. I would have gone to the gym every day of the week if I could. But like I said, my body was tired. After three months at the gym, I had to do a cost versus benefit analysis of continuing this thing I loved. Working out at the gym should have been good for me, but it was overloading my body with stress. I chose to listen to my body and made the incredibly hard decision to leave. My body needed time to recover. Just one day after making the decision to stop going to that particular gym, I threw out my back doing the dishes. I didn't lift anything heavy; I didn't even bend over to grab anything. I was washing one of my son's plastic cups and was all of a sudden rendered useless.

Have you ever taken a vacation and immediately gotten sick? Or taken a day off work to get things done and felt so exhausted that you spent the whole time in bed? Or in my case, made the decision to stop a physically taxing activity and immediately injured yourself doing something unrelated and far less strenuous? Dr. Marc Shoen, a psychologist and assistant clinical professor at UCLA's Geffen School of Medicine calls it the "Let-Down Effect."[27] Essentially, the stress that we have been inflicting on ourselves has an impact on our immune system. The stress hormones our body releases during high pressure seasons strengthens our immune system against illness. But when that stressful period ends, our immune system regulates and our body becomes more prone to sickness and injury. In other words, I had been applying so much stress on my body for so long that when I finally decided I needed to take some time off, my body seemingly shut down and decided I needed to spend a few weeks on the couch.

---

[27]https://www.kinatex.com/cliniques/dorval/en/uncategorized/the-let-down-effect-or-why-you-crash-after-a-period-of-prolonged-stress/

Yerkes-Dodson law states there is an optimal level of stress that helps to increase our performance.[28] A moderate level of stress is useful in helping us stay focused and engaged in what we are doing. Unfortunately, when there is too large of a surge of stress and anxiety, even when it's in pursuit of something that we want, we tend to lose that focus, and our ability to reach our potential decreases. In this case, even when we feel we're too committed to our goal to back off now, the overwhelm of stress starts to work against us, and it becomes too much to handle. I had clearly hit a level of stress and overwhelm that was no longer benefiting me.

After six weeks of very little physical activity because of my back injury, I finally felt better. I was ready to begin exercising again. I was ready to get back to my lifestyle of movement and healthy eating. Because, let's be honest, when you spend six weeks on the couch, your eating habits tend to take a dip (or a full on landslide) toward unhealthy.

That week my whole family got impetigo, a highly contagious skin infection that took turns running through everyone in my family. Twice. Soon after, my daughter and I got pink eye, which we happened to contract while already battling COVID. My daughter got an ear infection directly after that. We all took turns with the flu, and I, of course, got the longest stint of it. Less than a week later, I developed bronchitis.

During those three weeks of bronchitis, my grandpa became ill and spent four weeks in the hospital. I didn't want to get him sick, so I stayed away. This caused far too many flashbacks of my mom being in that same hospital and me not being able to visit her because of the COVID restrictions. My husband and I finally got to see him one Saturday afternoon. It was the first time in a long time my entire family was healthy for more than two days. He passed

---

[28] https://www.simplypsychology.org/what-is-the-yerkes-dodson-law.html

away that next Monday. Two days after my grandpa's funeral, my son came down with respiratory syncytial virus (RSV), which was going around our town with a vengeance at the time.

Do you ever just get tired of feeling like you have one excuse after another? If I could put emojis in a book, I would have the *hand-raised* emoji, right next to the *facepalm* emoji, inserted about 30 times over the last few paragraphs. Because even when you know that there will always be obstacles standing in the way of your goals, it's still easy to let life put those goals on the backburner.

During those really hard weeks of feeling like I wasn't able to come up for air, I was texting with a friend, and we were discussing the current state of our health goals. Here's my exact text to her: *My priorities have been on everything other than weight loss even though my weight gain is the number one thing on my mind, most of the time.* It's not even that exercise and health were pushed to the back burner because other things came first. I placed them on the back burner, intentionally. I knew that my family, my business, my book, my podcast, and all of the other things were going to take precedence over my health for the time being. But then I started to pull back from engaging with my family, my business, my book, and my podcast because I was fatigued. I was feeling sorry for myself that I didn't look and feel the way that I wanted to.

What had happened? Where did that relentless pursuit of habits and health go? At the beginning of this chapter, I talked about what it looks like to walk into the wind. When we put intentions toward something, it feels hard and there is resistance, so we have to try harder to make sure we keep course and walk deliberately toward our goal. When I took the intensity off of my health goals, it was like I had turned out of the wind. The resistance was still there, but instead of walking into it with clear and deliberate steps, I allowed it to propel me in the wrong direction. The intensity of all the things that come with being an adult started to propel me faster and faster *backward* toward my starting point—a destination I had not wanted to return to.

This is how I know the Foundation of Self wasn't a one-time phenomenon. I have been through the process of strengthening my Foundation of Self and all of the residual benefits that come with working on becoming the best version of myself, over and over again. I have also seen what happens when we stop taking control of the habits in the first tier. When we stop putting intentional action toward our physical and mental health, sleep, boundaries, mindset, etc., our foundation becomes unstable. I have seen what it looks like, and I wouldn't recommend it.

All of a sudden, my confidence was once again tied to certain things in my life and no longer something I felt I had control over. The moments of joy and gratitude felt fewer and farther between. My consistency, productivity, and discipline came into question. My authenticity started to feel compromised. I started to question my personal growth. *If I have truly grown, how did I let myself get back into this situation?* Weight loss is one example I use often because I believe many people can relate, but this concept can be applied to our businesses, careers, relationships, etc.

I've come to understand that we grow through the ebbs and flows of life and that growth strengthens the stability of our Foundation of Self. With every success, we grow. But even more so, with every mistake we make, every failure we encounter, and every moment of embarrassment or frustration that we endure, we grow.

When I was explaining my frustration to my doctor, I jokingly asked her for some sort of medication or something to get me back to "myself." I told her how frustrated I was. I explained that I knew exactly how to fix what I was feeling, but it's so much harder to turn back into the wind with strength and focus after being propelled by it for so long. Often, the effort is too great, and we decide against it.

I needed a good kick in the butt, but if I couldn't be tough enough on myself to turn things around, I didn't know what she could possibly do to help me. Then she said probably the only thing that would do the trick, "You are aware of it." She didn't try to talk me out of my feelings. She didn't berate me for my choices, even though I directly asked her to. She validated what I was saying and encouraged me to continue to dig into my feelings. Suddenly, I permitted myself space for the feelings to continue to surface. Instead of pushing them out of my head and creating yet another excuse, I began to encourage them—not to make myself feel bad—to truly understand where my priorities were and if I needed to reevaluate them.

I always say that the right books and the right authors will choose you in the moment that you need them most. The same week that I saw the doctor about feeling overwhelmed and slightly depressed, I recorded a podcast episode with a friend of mine who recommended the book *Essentialism: the disciplined pursuit of less* by Greg McKown. That friend recommended the book as one that everyone needs to read for a healthier and more well-rounded life. I knew I had the book in my Audible library, and it had been there for a while. This also wasn't the first time I had someone recommend the book to me. However, this time it felt like the book was choosing me.

Essentialism had the message I needed to hear. But I needed to be willing to listen. It gave me permission to go back to basics, encouraging and reminding me that it doesn't need to be a one-size-fits-all approach. Eliminating the nonessentials would help me regain focus and clarity on my goals.

My foundation felt like it was a candle flickering in the wind. There was stress and frustration and on any given morning I wasn't sure if it would be a good day or a bad day. I didn't know if I would find joy in my tasks and responsibilities for the day, or if I would become frustrated and essentially dig myself deeper into the hole. Then I remembered that happiness is still there despite not being able to depend on its constant presence. (I will dig deeper into this concept in the next chapter.)

Piece by piece and habit by habit, I was able to begin rebuilding my Foundation of Self stronger than before. I was able to set some goals for myself that aligned with what I had been feeling the last few months, what I had been reading, what I had learned over the last 30 years, and what I had studied over the past six years. My favorite thing about the Foundation of Self is that it's very forgiving. We will never "finish" building, and that's the beauty of it, but it will also always be available to us. We will always have an opportunity to continue building (and in this case rebuilding).

There is a lesson here beyond understanding this process on a personal level. If we desire to be leaders, we must remember that we are responsible for being an example to others. When we choose to walk into the wind and do things requiring more work than most people are willing to do, we are *demonstrating determination*. The resilience we build through the process of improving ourselves sets a great example for our kids, employees, friends, family, etc. That's what will make us effective leaders!

One day, I was expressing some of my frustrations to my chiropractor. He happens to be someone who has high expectations for himself—something that we have in common—so what he said in response to my frustrations surprised me. He said, "I think this is good for you. Going through adversity will help you to have more grace for those who are also going through hard things. It will help you to be more relatable and understanding when people are not able to meet your expectations." His response is ultimately what made me feel compelled to share this story with you. It would have been really easy for me to share only the highlights and lessons that lead to building the Foundation of Self and skip sharing what it looks like when it gets shaky.

Leadership isn't just about showing our accomplishments and setting high expectations for those to follow, leadership is also about understanding the need to be vulnerable and continue leading through the good and the bad seasons. If we're willing to share the trial-by-fire moments in our lives, it makes us more relatable to those who feel like they're in the throes of life's difficulties by themselves. When we're willing to show our weaknesses, we can inspire others to turn hard things into their superpower. Not only will it help us to inspire others on an individual level, but, as leaders, we will be much more credible when helping our teams communicate through challenges. Being able to show that we know what it looks like to work our way out of a hard situation is more valuable than just telling them. When we can bring our team's challenges with us, we can learn what it looks like to motivate them and encourage them to work together to overcome the hard times.

Ultimately, the process of building our Foundation of Self is going to have many ups and downs. It will not always appear like we're making a lot of progress. Sometimes it will look like we're going backward, so much so that we'll question if we'll ever be able to turn it around. This is our one life. We have to take responsibility to make it look the way that we want it to, so we can say, *I did everything I could.*

CHAPTER 7: BRINGING GROWTH TO LIFE

"Happiness is a complicated subject because everyone's different. But if there's a common denominator in happiness—a universal fuel of joy—it's that people want to control their lives."[29]
- Morgan Housel

Let's review:

Tier one focuses on self-engagement. The habits we can incorporate to build a strong foundation. We have control over the habits we introduce into our lives and the priorities we set for ourselves in any given season of life.

Tier two allows us to define, and redefine, success and the things that we want more of in life, solidifying our self-worth first and foremost, and then creating avenues to more joy, consistency, authenticity, patience, adventure, humor, etc.—all of which are within our reach.

Tier three is made up of trust, emotional intelligence, leadership, self-compassion, social intelligence etc. All of these are areas of growth that will never *feel* complete because we continue

---

[29] https://www.goodreads.com/quotes/11188140-i-can-do-whatever-i-want-today-people-want-to

growing in our *self-awareness,* which is where these qualities collide.

Just like the other tiers, trust and social and emotional intelligence are not the only things that make up this level of self-awareness. While they are three main areas of focus, this level is made up of all of the things we continuously work on, and in all reality, will never fully master.

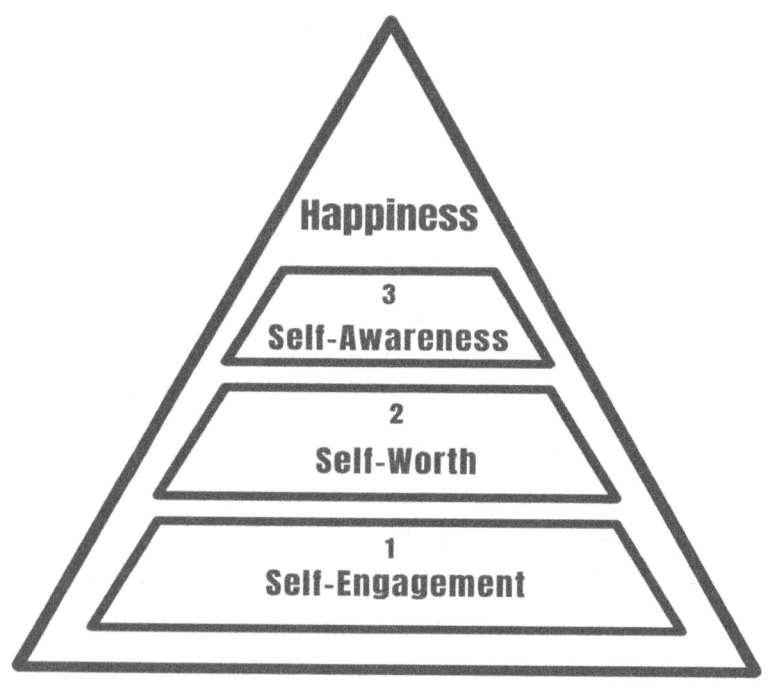

Foundation of Self

Self-awareness comes down to knowing ourselves better. When we can recognize and distinguish our thought patterns, we can begin to shift the way that we think. Asking ourselves the questions that get us closer to knowing what we want is also part of self-awareness. It comes down to being truthful and vulnerable with the answers we give ourselves. We become more self-aware with every new thing we learn about ourselves and the world around us, especially if it's something that we already know but can finally put into words. Then we can share it with others who also want to know us better.

Finding Happy 100 Percent of the Time

I spent a lot of time thinking about how to incorporate happiness into the Foundation of Self Framework. I'm guessing most people would assume that happiness is meant to be at the top. It's the thing that everyone wants in life: for themselves, their children, and their loved ones. But it's important to understand that to simply place happiness at the top of the pyramid would make it appear out of reach. It would look as though there are a lot of hoops to jump through and a lot of contingencies to get to a place where we can finally be *happy*.

That is not the message here. I always say that you can *find happiness* 100 percent of the time. I understand that it sounds like I believe people shouldn't allow themselves to be angry, sad, frustrated, guilty, or to feel anything that makes them human in the first place. But that is not the case. Let's start by answering the question, *How do you define happiness*? I'm serious. Take the time before you read on to define what happiness looks like to you. The Oxford English Dictionary defines being happy as everything from showing pleasure and contentment to finding confidence and satisfaction in our situation.[30] Happiness is a fleeting feeling; we

---

[30] https://www.oed.com/search/dictionary/?scope=Entries&q=Happy

will not feel 100 percent happy all of the time, we have to leave room for our other emotions. To strive for happiness 100 percent of the time would be setting ourselves up for failure. However, we can *find* happiness 100 percent of the time. We can find happiness, contentment, satisfaction, and/or confidence in our situation at any given moment if we know the right questions to ask and where to look.

I strongly believe that there is always an opportunity to find happiness because I experienced it through my own painful events. Even through my son being in the NICU, and losing my mom, I still felt sparks of joy every day, and I felt grateful for what I had. Even when I was going through some hard moments, and happiness was sometimes difficult to find, it was still there, present in every moment, even if some moments were overshadowed by more negative feelings.

Even as I knew this to be true, I was having a hard time putting it into words that would inspire others. Then I read Morgan Housel's book, *The Psychology of Money: Timeless Lessons on Wealth, Greed, and Happiness.* I won't lie to you, the majority of the book was over my head (stocks and finances are definitely not my love language!). However, I did have some major takeaways from the book, and my knowledge of financial history felt more rounded, but it wasn't until I was transcribing the passages I had highlighted into my notebook that I got excited. I had read and highlighted something that would end up being exactly what I needed to finally put into words what I had been struggling to communicate. It was about *control*: having control over our state of mind, our habits, our health, our relationships, and most importantly, our time. We can't control the circumstances around us. We can't control how other people act, feel, and respond. And we can't control how society shifts from one year or decade to the next. We can only control how we respond, our mindset, and our role in every situation. Even in really hard moments, when we feel like we have no control, we can take a little back by modeling it for others. We can lead by example by learning to control ourselves; therefore, showing others how to control their emotions and respond more positively.

This was the first time I could combine all that I knew about happiness into something attainable for everyone. We can define happiness as a state of mind, something that even in times of sadness, anger, frustration, and grief, we can find joy and be grateful for what we have.

Happiness is not the end goal. Happiness is not a separate topic. As you can see, happiness encompasses everything. It is wrapped around the entire framework because that's what the framework is: finding happiness in building a life we love.

Bringing the Foundation of Self to the Workplace

Whether you follow the Enneagram, Clifton Strengths, The Four Tendencies, Human Design, Myers-Briggs, or the DISC method, there is one thing that all of the different personality assessment tools have in common: they all agree that every individual is unique. For example, introversion and extroversion are often viewed as *either/or* traits. You are either outgoing (extroverted) or shy (introverted). But we need to view these traits on a spectrum, where over seventy percent of the

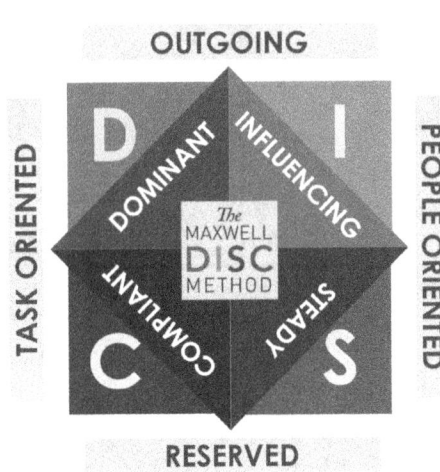

population fall somewhere in the middle.

This is also how we should view the different personality assessments. We are all on a spectrum of the different personality traits. I won't go into all of the different assessments, but I specifically want to dive a bit deeper into the DISC Method because I will be using it again in Chapter 8 when we discuss workplace culture. The DISC method is a personality assessment focused on workplace interactions that categorize individuals into one of four categories: dominant, influencing, compliant, and steady[31] (depicted in the graphic on the left). I will tell you that I am a high I/D on the DISC graph, which means that I am considered outgoing, dominant, and influential. If I used those assessments as an absolute, it would be easy to say that when I offend someone, it's because of my dominant (and sometimes abrasive) personality; it's just who I am. It would be easy for me to say that I have no patience for people who don't speak up and then complain they're never heard. It would be easy to say that anyone who doesn't like my "aggressively friendly" personality just isn't someone I should be spending time with. But, if instead, we use these assessments as a benchmark, we can begin to see what it looks like to view situations from other points of view, becoming more understanding and less judgmental of those we don't know.

For example, when I was managing the dementia facility, I would have been a much more effective leader if I had a better understanding of not just my assessment, but the assessment of those I was leading. A common trait of someone with my I/D personality is changing things quickly and often without much evaluation to confirm the change is in the best interest of those around them. I would have begun to understand that my leadership

---

[31]https://www.maxwellleadership.com/blog/understanding-your-communication-style/#:~:text=The%20idea%20behind%20The%20Maxwell,connect%20with%20others%20more%20effectively.

method was clashing with those of the nursing staff. It's pretty common for healthcare staff to have an S/C personality. They are steady, compliant, and often do not like change, let alone fast change for no reason. If we had spent the time to understand ourselves, and one another, better, we could have begun to work together as a team, rather than always trying to fix issues after the damage had been done.

These personality assessments can help us begin to understand ourselves and others better. This expanded view can grow our emotional and social intelligence, helping us meet people where they are. We can bring together all the personalities in a room and work through the different goals and agendas that are no doubt fighting against one another. We can begin to give a voice to every opinion. When we learn to leverage the entire spectrum of personality styles, we can begin to close the gaps between those who think they have nothing in common. (People usually have more in common than they think.) As leaders, we can use our personality to begin to change the conversation.

When we find ourselves in situations that feel out of our control, we can reclaim a feeling of happiness by finding something we do have control over. For instance, if we approach a conversation so it creates space for every person and personality style to be included, we're controlling the situation. This is true not only in the workplace, but with our family, friends, and in the community as well.

(If you would like to discover your own DISC personality, visit https://desireepetrich.com/disc)

You'll notice I used the words *start* and *begin* a lot in the last few paragraphs. I did this to reiterate that this process is ongoing; it will never fully be completed. We will all have opportunities to continue learning more about ourselves, as well as the other people in our lives. This is why my favorite services to offer as a leadership trainer are workshops. There is something so powerful in bringing people together in a safe and fun environment and hearing coworkers and their leaders share their appreciation and gratitude for one another. But more than that, it is creating an opportunity for people to have hard conversations in a fun and less intimidating environment than your typical staff meeting rather than waiting until conflict requires a trip to the HR office. We'll talk more about conflict in the next chapter, but the overarching message is: *conflict is necessary*. When we can use what we know about ourselves and those around us, conflict doesn't have to be avoided, it can be encouraged.

I have had people question me about why I believe it's so important to meet people where they are and to accommodate other people's personality styles. *Doesn't it put our own authenticity in jeopardy if we're bending to other people's needs?* There is some truth behind this question. But that's the whole point! Growing in our social and emotional intelligence means that we are adding value to people as our authentic selves. It's not about changing our truth to match other people's stories or to keep other people happy. It's not about keeping peace or letting the pursuit of peace overshadow our own opinions. We can show up with our thoughts and ideas, and encourage others to use their voice and share their thoughts. If we can show up with confidence, we can become comfortable with conflict, just as we become comfortable with silence. Being an effective leader means being self-aware enough to know which is needed in different situations.

The effort to help people grow their social and emotional intelligence in the workplace can feel like a time waster, and likely a lot more touchy-feely than leaders believe they should get with their staff, but this humanizes the workplace. In a 2023 study of 800 U.S. employees, it was found that 69.5 percent of employees would be happier if they had deeper connections with work colleagues and

77.6 percent consider workplace connection important in achieving a great company culture.[32]

Leaders have a responsibility to get people back to basics and focus on those relationships. As humans, we look for connection in everything we do; as leaders, we need to focus on creating space and opportunities that benefit employee relationships. Society as a whole is beginning to shift from the old belief that work and home life should be separate, that you should leave your home life at the door when you enter work, and that it doesn't matter if you hate your job because you can leave it behind to enjoy your nights and weekends at home (and we wonder why the majority of Americans dread Mondays).

We are entering into a society that wants to enjoy a home life, feel confident and proud of relationships and contributions at work, and be able to talk about them at either place, merging the two experiences. This is not true for everyone. There are individuals who don't want to merge the two, and that's OK, we need to respect their boundaries as well. Social intelligence means that we not only recognize those boundaries, but that we respect them.

Confidence versus Conceit

When I was in the process of developing my Foundation of Self Framework, I knew that there needed to be a separation between our own feelings of success and the way that we interact with our peers. In tier two, we define what it would look like for us to feel confident, authentic, honest, joyful, fearless, adventurous, etc. But that didn't cover a problem expressed to me during one of my first years teaching group fitness at our local YMCA.

---

[32] https://nectarhr.com/blog/workplace-connection-statistics#:~:text=1

Desiree Petrich

I had only been teaching Zumba (a type of dance fitness) for a few months when we had our first staff meeting. We were all sitting on the floor in the aerobics studio and had just gone over all of the expectations of being a group exercise instructor when our boss asked us to share how things were going for us. I shared how my style was different from the other instructor's. I was much more cardio-focused, higher intensity, and chose some really upbeat and fun songs. I had been told by people that they loved my class for the intensity of it.

I never directly put down the other dance fitness instructors, but it was clear to everyone in the room that I felt my approach was superior. My boss made this clear to me when she asked me to stay behind to discuss the fact that everyone in the room knew I felt I had the better class. She explained to me that although I wasn't attempting to belittle anyone, by portraying that I was the best, it came across as conceited and self-serving. Not to mention, it was rude to discuss someone in a room where that person was not able to defend himself.

Talk about a slap in the face! As a young twenty-something, it was hard to hear that they thought I was self-centered and everyone in the room was aware of it except for me. This was my first lesson in abundance versus scarcity. It is natural to assume that everyone should want the same things that we want. Our personality style, our preferences, our relationships, and our skills all combine to create a *best of* list, even if it's not conscious.

At the time, it didn't occur to me that there was a whole demographic that wanted someone else's style over mine. There were people who didn't like the intensity of my class and therefore didn't come. I never interacted with these people, so I was only seeing things from my point of view. I was only getting feedback from the people who did like my class because the ones who didn't, weren't there to tell me.

For some reason, I was stuck in a scarcity mindset. I felt that in order for me to feel like I was doing well at my job, I needed to feel like people liked me the best. A scarcity mindset it typically derived from fear. Fear that in order for one to win, another must lose. Fear that there isn't room for everyone, so we need to take as much as we can get before *it* runs out ("it" being anything from praise, to money, to a position, etc.).

An abundance mindset, on the other hand, is *knowing* that just because one person is succeeding doesn't automatically mean the other person is going to fail. Someone with an abundance mindset knows that just because one person uses his or her voice doesn't mean it will overshadow anyone else's. And just because there are two options, doesn't mean that one is superior to the other; they are just different. Being confident and having an abundance mindset means you recognize both options can be helpful. This mindset also allows people to make their own informed decisions and accept whatever the other person chooses. I stick my foot in my mouth *a lot*. I often catch myself being really aggressive and having to clarify things I said. I once got feedback on a survey from a ten-week program I was facilitating, that said, "Desiree has an interesting delivery style. Her passion is commendable, but it's rather forceful." This was a bit hard for me to digest. As someone who teaches about social intelligence, it was hard to get this feedback. I wanted to be liked by everyone. But here's the thing, you will never be for everyone.

I spent the first 25 years of my life molding myself into what everyone else wanted me to be. I held back my personality as much as I could and conformed to the likes and dislikes of whichever group I happened to be spending time with in the moment. Every once in a while, my personality would come out but it almost always came back to bite me in the ass. Unfortunately, these occurrences just solidified that it was better to hold back and do what I needed to do to be liked.

Through a lot of self-awareness, and an attempt to find the *real me,* I understood that I wasn't going to be for everyone. I knew that there were going to be people who didn't love my aggressive personality. But I also knew that showing up and being everything to everyone was providing me with a lot of friendly acquaintances, but no real friends. I wasn't allowing myself to be vulnerable with anyone because that would mean having to share my true thoughts, feelings, and personality with people. When we are not leading with confidence, self-trust, and an abundance mindset, we're likely leading with something else.

This is where we tie the different pieces of the third tier together. It's not only about how we regulate our emotions and show up for other people, it's also how we treat ourselves, what we say to ourselves, how we follow through on the things that we say we want for ourselves, and how (or *if*) we make ourselves a priority.

Trust

Self-confidence is not something that can be gained through outside recognition. Self-confidence is gained from a belief that we have all the tools we need to succeed, no matter the situation we're put in or the circumstances that feel out of our control. We figure out how to guide our self-talk in a way that makes us feel prepared to take on the day. Self-confidence is not a necessity in a manager, but it is paramount for becoming a good leader. This is why the process of learning to be in control of our emotions, external actions, and overall happiness is so important when leading in every area of our lives.

Trust is built on self-accountability, meaning we follow through on the promises we make to ourselves. This could also be described as discipline, but it's not as simple as saying *I'm going to do it no matter what because I said I was going to do it.* Instead, we get clear about the goals that we set for ourselves, define what it would look like to be successful in that goal, and put in the work to start to build credibility. Our feelings of joy, confidence, consistency, etc. are not tied to any title or habit, but instead, they are tied to our intentions and effort.

The third tier is not meant to be viewed as a goal we're trying to reach. Its presence is a reminder that through every action we take, conversation we have, and habit we work toward, we have an opportunity to grow into a more well-rounded person.

Building self-awareness is a lofty goal that on its own can feel unattainable and overwhelming. There is no checklist of exactly what one has to do to achieve self-awareness. Knowing that the process of growth will never truly end could be frustrating to some. It could come across as *If I can never truly win, what's the point in playing the game?* But, if we can find excitement in the process, if we can define not "what" we want to be five or ten years from now, but "who" we want to be, we can truly find joy in the process.

Below are a few practices to become more self-aware as a leader.

- Understand that you will get feedback; it's the nature of the beast. You are responsible for making sure that everyone else is responsible and being held accountable. That is a hard position to be in, and often requires that you practice accepting feedback with vulnerability and acceptance.

- Practice the art of reading a room and responding to people's weaknesses, as well as encouraging their strengths.

- Be intentional about doing more of the good things on the front end so you can do fewer corrective and uncomfortable things on the back end.

- Practice the art of questioning the first thought that comes into your head. Remember, we don't control our first thought, but we do get to control the thought that comes after and the actions that follow.

- Establish trust with others by being vulnerable, transparent, and willing to ask for help and by allowing yourself to make mistakes.

- Be available for others to ask for help, and be available and supportive to others when they inevitably make mistakes. Assume positive intent, practice humility, and remember to be yourself.

CHAPTER 8: INDIVIDUALIZING THE WORKPLACE

"The best way to cultivate connection with one another is to further individualize ourselves from each other."
- Desiree Petrich

People-pleasing gets a bad reputation, but does it for a good reason? We are all in the business of adding value to others, whether you are a CEO adding value to your employees and the company, a customer service specialist whose main responsibility it is to keep the customers happy, a stay-at-home parent who spends his or her days adding value to the children, or a middle manager who gets to add value to those they're working for and those who are working for them. We are all in the business of adding value to others. This requires that we indulge in some form of pleasing other people. If we want to keep our customers and clients happy, if we want to keep our family and our children happy, they need to be at the forefront of the decisions that we make and the actions we take.

However, if we show up as anything other than our true selves in our interactions with people, we begin to set standards that are going to be hard to maintain. It will be hard to build a foundation of trust with people because we are constantly changing our persona to match what we think people want from us. For example, thinking back to my first management experience, I was very direct with those I was leading, and although we've established this was a result of fear, the employees didn't know that this wasn't my actual personality. On the other hand, the tenants of the facility and their children thought I was the most accommodating, kind, level-headed, and God-fearing person.

So who was I? And how was I supposed to build trust with those I was working with if I didn't even know the answer to that question? It became exhausting to be a different version of myself depending on who I was with. Somewhere in between these two personalities was my true self, and I was determined to find it.

During the pandemic, I realized I couldn't fake it anymore. There were people, employees, coworkers, tenants, their families, and my family all depending on me to handle the situation with as much grace and transparency as I could manage. I needed help. Whether you believe in fate or not, to say the stars aligned for me in that season of life would be an understatement. Between the increased demands of my job, the fact that I had a six-month-old who needed me, my sudden desire to be as healthy as I could be, and the fact that I was reading around seven to eight books a month, something started to click into place. That hidden version of myself was coming out. I started to become more kind and gracious to those I was managing. I became a little more direct in the expectations of the facility when it came to the tenants and their families (I had to, I was the middle-man between the government's requirements and what our families had to endure during that time.) But, ultimately, what I was becoming was more *me*.

The interesting thing to note here is the process of becoming more emotionally and socially intelligent wasn't directly intentional. I put in the work to read, exercise, pray, practice, etc., but the self-awareness and the actual interactions with those around me didn't take a lot of effort to change because I had been changing internally, to the point where it became natural externally.

There will continue to be instances where we have to make decisions in the moment. Making these decisions while rooted in our authentic selves means making decisions based on intuition versus the logical mind. If we do the work of becoming more self-aware, our intuition will hold the answers that we need as long as we ask it the right questions.

When I was working as a part-time events coordinator for the chamber of commerce, I was in charge of a women's event that sold out of all 150 tickets to a shopping and ladies' night. The event was amazing, other than one thing: we ran out of food. It was in a new location and the food was catered in, so there was no way to make more. There would have been enough, except we gave the attendees dinner plates (because they better matched the aesthetic we were looking to create), but we were expecting them to take appetizer-sized portions. Turns out, when you give a woman a dinner plate ...

There were at least 30 to 50 women who were still in line to get food when the caterer told me that the food had run out. They told me to go up to the front and inform everyone that there would be no more food for the evening. They advised me not to apologize but to be very matter-of-fact. It felt wrong to not apologize for this. Whether it was my fault or not, I was the leader of the event, and the responsibility was mine. I wrestled with whether or not to follow their advice about holding back my apology. I wish I could tell you I went with my gut and apologized in front of the 150 women about the food situation. Instead, I followed someone else's advice.

When we received the survey results back a few weeks later, my concerns were confirmed. There were very few people who complained that we had run out of food. They understood that things happen, especially in a new space. The complaints that we received were about my lack of an apology. These complaints came not only from the people who didn't get to eat that night but also the people that did.

The thing about making mistakes is that you get the opportunity to learn from them. You get the opportunity to be transparent and apologize for them. You get the opportunity to forgive yourself and move on. You get the opportunity to make sure you never make that mistake again. The best lessons often come from the things that you wish wouldn't have happened. But then, how would you grow?

Let's just say, I learned two important lessons.

1. Always apologize with authenticity if you feel like the situation warrants it. It does not show weakness to apologize. It shows empathy and an understanding of the situation at hand.

2. Always plan for more food than you think you'll need!

If I had separated myself from the embarrassment and frustration of the situation, I likely would have followed my intuition, rather than my logical mind, and apologized. If I would have allowed myself to pause for a moment and looked at every one of the 150 women as individuals, maybe my apology would have made a difference in their reaction to the situation. It wouldn't change the facts, but it would have made them feel seen and heard.

I've talked a lot about the benefits of further individualizing yourself from others, but what does that ultimately look like? Why does it make any difference in a team setting if the members of that team are viewed as individuals, rather than one entity, and treat one another as such?

A few stories come to mind ...

When I ultimately decided to leave the dementia care facility, it wasn't because I was burnt out from COVID-19, it was because I was exhilarated by it! The team I got to be a part of handled the situation with as much grace as one could hope to based on our circumstances. I was already in the highest position I could be in that facility, so how was I going to continue to grow if I stayed? (Unless there happened to be another pandemic, which I was really hoping would not be the case!)

I received an interview request from one of the jobs I applied for, and in that request, the owner of the company sent me a link to take a DISC assessment, the same one I had taken before (mentioned a few pages earlier). The assessment's purpose is to provide more self-awareness and insight for the individual, as well as to create common language and understanding for teams to use to improve teamwork. When I received the DISC results, I remember laughing out loud. My D (direct/dominant) point and my I (Influencing/Interactive) point on the graphs had completely flip-flopped. Over three years, I had switched my work personality from someone who approached a situation with directness, and what others would likely deem aggression, to entering each situation with an interest in people and desiring to add value wherever I found myself.

I was excited and proud to see this change. The result of the DISC assessment felt more aligned with who I felt like I was becoming and who I wanted to be. I am OK being a bit aggressive, I think it has served me well in my life. But ultimately, I want to enter every situation with the people as my main objective. I am also OK with a bit of people-pleasing, but everything I know to be true requires that I'm still honest and willing to be transparent and *direct* with people.

I realized after taking the second DISC assessment that the changes I had intentionally made throughout the past few years could be seen on paper, as well as in my relationships. From that realization, I fell in love with the DISC personality assessment. I love helping people analyze why they do what they do. I love helping individuals understand their teammates better and how they can augment one another's strengths and weaknesses so the team and the company can thrive. I love watching the shock and amusement on someone's face when they read through their DISC assessment results and chuckle at how closely the test pegged their personality and tendencies.

I always come back to two specific instances of working with teams that pretty well sum up the reason behind a lot of conflict within teams. In the bestselling book, *The Anatomy of Peace: Resolving the Heart of Conflict*,[33] by the Arbinger Institute, the author describes the difference between conflict and collusion. Conflict is something that is said externally that we react to (typically negatively), while collusion is based on the idea that we invite the exact behavior from our counterparts that we are complaining about.

Whether I'm leading a workshop, leading a small group session, or am one-on-one with a coaching client, collusion is the most recognized form of conflict, though most have never had a name to attach to it, or a good enough understanding of what it was to rectify it.

Let me explain.

I was working with individuals on a leadership team, all of whom happened to be women. I was a bit taken aback when analyzing their DISC reports in preparation for my one-on-one meetings with them the following week. All of their DISC reports showed a combination of the same two personality traits: C (compliant/controlled) and S (steady/stable). Both of these traits

---

[33]https://arbinger.com/store/the-anatomy-of-peace/

are described as *passive*, both of these traits indicate that the individual is process-oriented and doesn't typically like change, specifically rapid change. A majority of the women had S as their highest point (as does 69% of the populations), which means that they are loyal and can often be known as people-pleasers because they are people-oriented and attempt to avoid conflict.

The reason I found this interesting is because, typically teams are made up of all of the different styles, not necessarily by design but by coincidence. People are hired to augment the weaknesses of the other team members. This team, outside of their CEO, all held the same strengths. I didn't know what I would uncover when I talked with the team, but what I found would change the way I look at team dynamics in terms of their cohesiveness and their ability to love what they're doing and their team.

I worked one-on-one with each of the team members to discuss their DISC reports. Someone said something during the first assessment that made me ask the question, "What do you think is the thing that is hindering your team's ability to be the best it can be?" Her response was "trust." This made me ask the same question to the next few. "What is your team missing to be successful?" "Trust" was the answer that came up again. It came up for every person on that team.

As I continued having one-on-one discussions, another common theme was emerging. They would tell me that they were just trying to make everyone happy. They didn't want to hurt anyone's feelings. They didn't want to cause any conflict if they could help it. Some were new to the organization, so they didn't want to ruffle feathers. Some had been with the organization for a while, and they just wanted to give everyone a chance to get settled. They'd probably figure it out eventually.

So what was the problem? *They were all being too nice to one another!*

I spoke of the difference between conflict and collusion earlier in this chapter. This is the perfect example of inviting the behavior from people that we are ultimately complaining about. These women said that they were lacking trust, and I knew why. No one was saying what they meant. They would ask one another questions about projects just so they could form a connection, but they didn't actually need help because they already knew the answer. This would frustrate the person they asked for help from because they didn't take their suggestion, or advice, and it would look like they just didn't like the answer they got.

Team members were avoiding their projects because, to complete them, a small amount of conflict would be necessary. Everyone was being nice to one another, so on the outside, it didn't appear as though anything was wrong. But every team member was frustrated by the lack of connection between them. No one trusted the other to be honest. They were all inviting people-pleasing and a lack of transparency from one another, but this was the exact thing that they were complaining about in regards to one another.

There is one thing everyone who engages in this type of conflict has in common - they are leading from fear. There is a pattern that keeps showing up again and again as I work with teams. Fear amplifies our most innate traits. In my case, as someone with a more direct personality, my fear was showing up as aggression. In my mom's case, where she had more of a stable and loyal personality, her fear was an amplified version of people-pleasing and she ended up doing everything for everyone.

The best way to approach collusion (the less obvious type of conflict), or to counteract it, is to individualize ourselves. We can't assume that our approach will look anything like someone else's.

The better we know our team and employees, the more easily we can identify and define what fear and conflict look like for them. Fear comes across in so many different ways. Avoiding direct conflict may seem noble because we don't want to hurt other people's feelings (and we don't want our own feelings to be hurt), but it ultimately leads to collusion (the type of conflict that can be hard to recognize and overcome).

As a leader, this is where social intelligence comes into play. If we start to see (or sense) this type of conflict, we need to take responsibility to engage and encourage conversation, even if it leads to another type of conflict (the productive kind!). As leaders, it is our responsibility to invite an opinion from those who are quiet and may not interject, even though they have something to say. If we know that an individual doesn't like being put on the spot, we can prep the conversation by saying that we will be asking each person's individual take on the matter. This will give the person time to formulate an answer, and although he or she may feel uncomfortable engaging in the conversation at the moment, it's important for that person's voice to be heard and that they feel acknowledged as part of the team.

Collusion is a bit inconspicuous as it's bubbling below the surface, but sometimes, conflict just looks like conflict. That's what we're dealing with in the next team example.

Two employees didn't like the way a new manager was taking the reins. Projects with a lower level of importance were suddenly made the priority and non-urgent matters were resulting in 15 emails by 10 a.m. This is the definition of micromanaging. I had already spoken to the new manager. I knew her personality style. I knew the excitement and fear that went into everything she was doing. I knew the frustration that she had with her coworkers. I knew her backstory and her history of enduring abuse. I knew that this was the first time in her life that she had begun to feel confident. I knew that her high C (compliant) personality was causing her to feel anxious when people didn't respond to her, which then caused her to send multiple emails very close together. I also knew that her personality was causing this project to feel like the most important thing in her mind. She wanted to do her job, and she wanted to do it well. I knew she was scared. I knew that she was leading in her new position out of a place of fear. I could see how badly she wanted to keep her newfound air of confidence by getting the job completed as quickly and as accurately as possible. Reading between the lines, I could see that she was frustrated that no one seemed to be taking this project as seriously as she was.

When I asked the other employees what they thought the new manager's personality style was, they said there was no doubt she was a high D. She was demanding, direct, micromanaging, and aggressive. Despite being slightly offended as a person with a high-D personality style, I could see exactly where they were coming from. If I had spoken to them first and didn't already know her personality style, I may have even been persuaded to join their *side*.

I have explained fear as a response to conflict multiple times, but this time felt even more crucial to get right. When we lead from a place of fear, our natural tendencies can be amplified to a point of unbalance. In other words, her natural tendencies as someone who really likes rules and regulations and appreciates accurate information became aggressive in her pursuit of a completed project. Her desire to have everything perfect resulted in an overabundance of excitement in making sure that she had everything she needed. This lack of social awareness put a strain on the employees whom she was calling on for help.

Through the teams' coaching sessions, we determined ways for the manager to come back to a place of peace and confidence in getting the project done well, without upsetting any of the employees. The employees were able to see the project from her point of view and began to understand why she had gotten so focused on something that, to everyone else, seemed inconsequential. I spoke with the manager of this team one week after we wrapped up our meetings, and she expressed how well two specific members of the team had been working together. They were being respectful of one another's approaches to their projects and even joined forces to take on another project. Their strengths combined to make the perfect team.

Our strengths are a great tool, but so are our weaknesses. If for no other reason than they help us understand ourselves and one another on a deeper level, holding more grace for one another as we work to make the team and the company as successful as we can. As vulnerable and scary as it may feel to open up and share our insecurities with our coworkers, it can also be the thing that can create a level of trust you may never get otherwise.

There is one last point I want to make on this matter, specifically in regard to what happens when we don't define why someone is acting in a manner that isn't adding value to the others on a team. How many times have you either heard, or seen, a story where several employees quit a company because of one individual? Maybe that person is rude, aggressive, and puts down their employees. Maybe it's someone who is perfectly pleasant one moment, and the next, no one knows why that person is so pissed off. Maybe it's someone who micromanages and berates employees to the point they feel like they can't do anything right, and they won't ever gain their trust.

If one of the individuals who quit was telling their friend about the experience, they would likely say something about how the company has a bad culture. *How could the managers not see what's going on? How can they not fire this person causing all of these problems?*

Desiree Petrich

I have seen it time and time again: people quit their jobs because of one individual without ever telling their manager. They assume the issue is apparent, and they don't need to cause additional conflict among the team by bringing it up again. The individuals *causing issues* are typically high achievers. They might not understand how they are coming across. Their managers don't see anything other than effective work from them, especially if no one else is willing to come forward and express their concerns. By the time the fifth employee has quit, and a pattern starts to arise, it feels like it's too late to approach the individuals causing the issues without risking so much conflict that it will be hard to come back from.

Company culture is made up of every individual on the team and in the company. Every employee needs to take on the responsibility for their own voice and for those on their team. While it's important to ask how leaders can invest in their employees, the responsibility still comes back to the individual. If we're having a concern with a coworker, it's our responsibility to speak up (we expect this of our kids if they're getting bullied; that responsibility doesn't change when we enter the workforce). If we want others, specifically our companies, to invest in us, then we have to work hard, create a succession plan for what we'd like to see for our future, and engage our bosses to help build the skills we need to move through that growth plan. We have to ask for what we want!

Any individual in a company can be defined as a leader. A leader is someone who encourages engagement in those around them. Leaders are those who inspire others and work to build connections amongst the employees on a team. Leaders are those who recognize others on their team for their positive attitudes and their hard work. Good leaders are those who go even further and figure out how each individual prefers to be recognized. Different personality types prefer recognition in different ways. I like when people shout it from the rooftops; some prefer a quiet email that doesn't require making a scene. Knowing each other's personalities is critical to good leadership and a healthy team.

Recognizing that teams and companies are made up of individuals could be taken too far and could potentially backfire. If we're not having the conversation on a regular basis, people could misinterpret individuality as an opportunity to focus only on their work, neglecting to help those who need it. It's important as a leader to have the conversation about why we are focusing on the individual. We focus on the individual to humanize them and remind ourselves we shouldn't be focusing solely on our individual work but on the priorities of the team. It helps open the doors for transparency, which develops a level of trust and accountability between team members. It is important to have ongoing conversations about the fact that while the team is made up of individuals, each of those individuals is responsible for the success of the team.

Our happiness at work is based on our perceived value, not how our value is perceived by others. It is more how each of us *interprets* our value to be perceived by others. Our happiness is directly tied to the connection to those around us. Confidence at work is tied to the goals we set for our career, whether it's to get promoted all the way to the top or simply be the best employee that we can be.

CHAPTER 9: EVERYTHING ELSE

"If you don't like something, change it. If you can't change it,
change your attitude."[34]
- Maya Angelou

I have had my share of personal learning experiences in my career and my personal life. I have gained and lost the weight. I've been a bad manager, and I've worked my way to being a good leader. I've had bad managers and had to try and lead from behind. I've had great managers and was able to follow their advice and example. I was the person who didn't like how I was showing up and put in the work to close the gap between where I was and where I wanted to be. I've also had some incredible lows and life experiences that made everything I was working on feel like it wasn't worth the time. But the greatest thing that I've had is a desire to *do* more and *be* more. I feel very fortunate to have developed a love of reading. I have learned a lot as a result of navigating outside circumstances and building resilience and grit along the way. But even more than that is what I've learned from the books and authors that I have been fortunate enough to invite into my world.

We can read as much as we want and ask for and receive endless advice, but, ultimately, it's up to us to do the work. The changes we make in life and the confidence we acquire along the way are a result of our openness to try new things, get out of our

---

34 https://www.harpersbazaar.com/culture/features/a9874244/best-maya-angelou-quotes/

comfort zone, meet new people, and work hard to continue building a life we love.

I haven't addressed work-life balance in this book because it's not a concept I have lived by. I want to be well-rounded and to integrate these parts of my life. I want to enjoy my work enough that I'm OK bringing it home every once in a while. I want to be able to have a (mostly positive) conversation about my work with my spouse. I want to be able to bring my personal life to work. I want to know my coworkers and their lives, just as I want them to know mine. Living this way hasn't always been easy. Some jobs made it really hard to not complain to my spouse; some jobs made it hard to make friends at work because of the competitive nature of the job; some jobs were not sustainable because they didn't allow me to bring my home life to work and build a level of trust and respect with my coworkers.

I believe that every single experience is a good one even if it didn't feel that way at that moment. We may not be able to immediately say, *at least it will be a good lesson later*, but the ability to see every mistake, every failure, every relationship (good or bad), and every experience as a lesson is a skill that we have to learn and a muscle we have to flex. It's a mindset shift that may take a while to grasp but could ultimately change our lives for the better.

Our purpose and passions may change. Some relationships will grow and flourish, while others fade away. Some memories will be looked back on with a smile and some with a chuckle and a shake of our heads. But one thing remains true: if we choose to view each of these as an opportunity, we'll never lose the lessons that we learn along the way.

There are some concepts that have been life-changing for me but don't require an entire chapter. I decided there was no way that

I could leave these things out. So, here are ten of my absolute favorite tools and mindset shifts I use to elevate my influence as a leader. Some of these are gentle reminders that I like to keep front and center in my life, while others are reminders that hit me hard when I feel like I'm getting knocked down, and they never fail to help build me back up.

Ten Tools and Mindset Shifts to Build Trust and Instill Confidence in Ourselves and Our Teams

1. The Checkmate Rule

In my keynote speech, "5 Rules for Life," one of my rules is called Checkmate. The key concept is to remember that we are playing the long game. We have to strategically place ourselves in situations that will give us the best opportunity to succeed. We need to think a few steps ahead. We have to take into account that every person has a different point of view, a different set of experiences, and a different approach to the various situations we find ourselves in at any given time.

Regardless of who we are and where we are on our journey, we all have a desire to succeed. The definition of what that ultimately looks like is specific to each of us. What does it look like to *succeed*? The second tier of the Foundation of Self not only allows, but encourages, us as individuals to define what success looks like in different areas of our life. What would it look like for us to feel like we reached our potential? Will we ever know? Is the definition of *potential* forever expanding, or is it a solid definition that we can work toward?

Those are questions we have to answer for ourselves. Understanding there is a path in front of us that needs to be navigated with intention can help to breathe new life into days that feel long (even though the years feel short).

2. Building Confidence Is as Easy as ABC

Even when I try something new, even when it feels like I'm a million miles outside of my comfort zone, I still don't have to build my confidence from scratch.

I love working with high school and college students. I share a level of naivety with them that helps us to connect. But one thing I get asked over and over again from those between the ages of 17 and 25, is some form of the question, *How do I build my confidence?* This question is a bit like asking, *What is the best way to serve eggs?* I could tell them how I like my eggs, but that's just one person's opinion.

I could tell them what I think it takes to build confidence, but the process is 100 percent up to the individual to answer. However, when I answer their very serious question with a half-assed answer, it doesn't always translate well. So, I've started to answer with this, "Building confidence is as easy as ABC: acquisition, belief, and consistency."

The ABCs

Acquire skills by trying new things. Leaving our comfort zone doesn't need to look like throwing caution and common sense to the wind. Our goals should play a large role in the new skills we're looking to acquire. Who do we need to know, and what do we need to learn in order to keep moving forward? We get to decide our specific skills and spced, as long as we're not standing still. Your confidence will continue to grow as you acquire new skills and new relationships.

If you're stuck for ideas, revisit the first tier of the Foundation of Self Framework and dive into the different categories. Pick one and start there! Or visit desireepetrich.com/framework, and we can do it together during a live workshop.

Believe in our own abilities. The imaginary finish line between where we are and the things we want is one that we have to *choose* to cross. There is no single event that can make us believe it, and another person's words won't make the difference. It's a decision that we get to make to show up as someone who knows they have the tools to maneuver within any situation they come across.

Cultivate **Consistency** by practicing skills. Reinforce positive thoughts and actions. Trust ourselves to do what we say we're going to do. Following through consistently helps solidify our belief in ourselves.

Circling back to the Foundation of Self Framework, we remember that confidence is only one thing that needs to be defined. This ABC framework can be used to help us define and work toward anything that we want more of ... joy, adventure, humor, authenticity, transparency, etc.

It's as easy as ABC. Try to remember that very few things are life and death. It's OK to try new things; it's OK to try and fail. And, who knows, we may just learn something!

3. Answer Immediately

I was having a conversation with someone who has an S (stable), and C (compliant) personality. In other words, this person is on the passive side of the DISC profile. He said one of his greatest barriers to feeling like a good leader is that he tends to take too long to respond to people. He'll get an email with a question or request, and he freezes because he wants to answer correctly.

This is a two-part lesson.

The greatest fear for someone with a C-style personality is typically a fear of criticism. In other words, he was leading from a place of fear. He would take a long time to respond to emails and requests from coworkers because he wanted the answer to be perfect, but what they ultimately were upset about was his lack of timeliness to even acknowledge that he received the request. It made him feel like an inconsistent leader. Understanding this about himself, we were able to brainstorm a few approaches that would help his coworkers feel like he was responding in a timely manner. It would help him feel like he wasn't leaving people hanging while also putting in the time he felt the question/request deserved.

The trick is this: *answer immediately*.

We don't have to answer in a way that completes the task at hand, especially if answering quickly would be stressful. If we're working with others, most of the time they just want to know that we've received their message. Answer immediately. Simply responding quickly will buy some time for us to give a more thoughtful answer. My typical *immediate answer* is something along the lines of:

Thank you, I received your email and will get back to you with an answer. Do you have a deadline as to when you need this information, so I can ensure I am timely with my response?

This lets the sender know I have received the email. It puts the ball back in the sender's court to give me additional details and allows the person to follow up with me (if I haven't responded by the due date they gave) without feeling like a nag.

Answering immediately helps us feel more in control and less pressured to complete their request. This trick is one that I use often. My personality style isn't one that would get stressed about keeping someone waiting, but it's a tool I've picked up over the years as a way to build trust with others. By keeping them up to date, they feel seen and heard regarding their conversations and interactions with us. Anything that we can do to continue to build on our relationships is going to help build trust with those we're working with.

4. Inevitability Mindset

The inevitability mindset can have both positive and negative associations, so let me define the difference.

Inevitability could look like someone avoiding dating because they assume it's inevitable that it won't work out, and it's not worth trying. Believing that changing jobs will result in another bad experience because it's inevitable that the grass will *not* be greener on the other side is another example of a negative mindset around inevitability.

I have been at a place in life where I used inevitability as an excuse to not go for what I wanted. But I have also been able to use the positive approach to an inevitability mindset. I started my business with the mindset that it will not fail. I may fail along the way but regardless of what my business looks like in the end, it will not be a failure. This mindset has helped me to maintain a level of consistency that would not be possible if I were waiting for it to come crashing down with every step.

Some people may call this *toxic positivity* (an unwillingness to believe that bad things happen), but it's not denial, and it's not avoidance. My inevitability mindset is based out of optimism and knowing that every trial and error will bring a lesson. This will inevitably help me to overcome any obstacle that is placed in my way.

When I listened to Simon Sinek's audiobook, *The Infinite Game*, there was one concept that helped me solidify the idea that an inevitably mindset is not about rigidity, but about flexibility with an end goal in mind. The message boiled down to this; growth should not be seen as a finite metric. It is a variable that sometimes needs to be fast, and sometimes needs to be approached more slowly to ensure that it lasts.[35]

I don't know what the future is going to look like. I don't know who will be beside me along the way, but I know I am willing to be flexible in my pursuit of creating a business that I love, one that will create an environment of hope and optimism for all who enter the dream.

---

[35] Sinek, Simon. 2019. *The Infinite Game*. Penguin Audio.

5. Abundance Mindset

Do you feel that for one person to win another has to lose? Or is there enough room for everyone? I have already covered what it means to have an abundance mindset, but I want to share a specific example that will help you understand why I'm so persistent about this approach.

There is someone in town who owns a business pretty similar to mine. In the past, I would have considered him to be a competitor and likely tried to distance myself from what he was doing. (Similar to when your coach tells you not to watch an opponent too closely or you'll get psyched out). Instead, I took an abundance mindset approach, and I asked him to meet for coffee. We shared ideas and resources and told one another our stories of adversity that ultimately led us to this point. Six months after that first coffee, I asked him to be a part of my first leadership conference. I wanted to create an opportunity where we could continue to work together. Shortly after, he presented me with an opportunity to work together that would be a huge shift in my business strategy going forward.

So was this a sign that I asked for that came to fruition *because* I was asking for it? Was it just two people with abundance mindsets offering opportunities to one another because of the value and respect we hold for one another?

Yes and yes!

I encourage you to view your day, your week, and your life with an abundance mindset. Invite others to the conversation. Ask for their thoughts and opinions. Know that your willingness to include them will only make you more of a leader at work and in life as you continue to add value to others.

6. Responsible *to* Not *For*

I will likely fight this mindset for the rest of my life. It's possible that being the oldest child created a need for me to keep everyone safe, make sure no one's feelings get hurt, and help everyone reach their maximum potential, whether they feel any pull to do so or not.

Feeling responsible for people almost stopped me from starting my own business. I wanted so badly to help people that I didn't know if I could handle coaching people who say they want to change but don't take any intentional action toward helping themselves.

It's hard when someone asks for advice, we give it to them, and he or she does nothing with it. It's hard when someone complains about problems incessantly but is unwilling to do anything about a solution. It's hard to see someone not living up to his or her full potential because of fear, complacency, or feeling trapped.

One concept changed all of that for me. At first, it felt incredibly selfish, and to be honest, sometimes it still does feel a bit selfish, but it allows me to view my relationships from another angle.

I am responsible to people, not for people.

From a quick glance, those two things don't seem all that different from one another, but the slight difference is enough to keep my sanity! Taking responsibility *for* someone else is futile. We cannot determine the way people will behave or respond. We can't control who they spend their time with, or what they spend their time doing. We can't hear their thoughts; we can only see their actions.

Being responsible *to* someone else brings the responsibility back to us by recognizing what part we should play in the relationship and fulfilling *only* those obligations. Being responsible involves holding *ourselves* accountable and following through on the commitments we make.

Being responsible to others requires that we know who we are and what our values are. We need to take responsibility to be honest and transparent while both talking *and* listening.

Here's the thing: we are surrounded by others who we can't control from our parents to our children and from our superiors to our employees. We are not able to control their behaviors or anything else about them, for that matter. We don't have to be OK with everything they do or say, but we can't waste our energy trying to get others to meet our expectations. When we can pull back—remembering that our responsibility is limited to the interactions we have with that person—we can move on from being fixated on another person's outcomes and focus on being the absolute best version of ourselves.

There is one final point that I think sums up this entire concept: there is nothing wrong with wanting people to change. It can be hard to watch the people we love go through things we know we could have helped them avoid or not do things we know would help them get to their goals faster. It can be hard to accept that we have no control, especially when our boss won't change the way things *have always been done*, even though we can see a better way, or when our coworkers are not taking on their portion of the workload.

It is not a problem to want them to change. The problem is insisting others change while we are unwilling to consider how we may be contributing to the problem. Before looking outward, we need to *identify the problem* and take responsibility for fixing what we can.

Empathy is another important aspect of feeling responsible *to* people. We need to be willing to look at things from another person's point of view, not just from a behavioral perspective but from a situational sense, without feeling responsible *for* their choices. Changing the way we think about our responsibility to others can help promote a sense of mutual respect and trust in the relationship. We won't feel like we need to "fix" others' problems for them, but we will be there leading by example and willing to listen when they need us.

Changing the way I think about my responsibility to myself and others changed everything for me. Like I said, it can feel selfish to look at relationships and only focus on ourselves, releasing the need to take on other people's motivations, behaviors, and actions. But doing so will release stress and strain on a relationship not only in our minds but in theirs as well. Our objective needs to be letting them know we're there to help if they need it and following through on our end of the deal by being the best version of ourselves.

7. Full-Time Energy

When I was working part-time as an events coordinator, I surprised people often when I told them that I was only working 24 hours a week. One person followed up their surprise by exclaiming, "But you have such full-time energy!"

A few weeks after her comment, I had an opportunity to ask her what she meant. She said that the persistence and consistency I had to follow up with people, as well as the energy I had when running the events, was contagious and made her feel really welcomed and included. This conversation has stuck with me as a reminder that regardless of the commitment we have made to something, we can always go above and beyond the requirements of that responsibility by showing up as our best selves.

Having come from a full-time leadership position where a lot of responsibility for tenants, families, employees, the building, and the reputation of a facility was on my shoulders, it would have been so easy to view a position with much less responsibility, fewer hours, and less pay as an opportunity to take it easy, caring less about the outcome. I would like to believe that caring less is not in my DNA, but a book I was reading during my transition between jobs illustrated to me what it means to be committed, regardless of the size of the commitment. One quote, in particular, stuck with me. Martin Luther King Jr. said, "If a man is called to be a street sweeper, he should sweep streets even as Michelangelo painted, or Beethoven composed music, or Shakespeare wrote poetry. He should sweep streets so well that all the hosts of heaven and earth will pause to say, 'Here lived a great street sweeper who did his job well.'"[36]

In my role as a part-time events coordinator, I was not responsible for people. I wasn't responsible for making people attend the events. I wasn't responsible for making

---

[36] https://www.goodreads.com/quotes/21045-if-a-man-is-called-to-be-a-street-sweeper

people learn something, and I wasn't responsible for making them enjoy the experience. I was responsible for showing up as the best version of myself as I could and planning the events to the best of my ability.

If my "calling" was to be a part-time events coordinator, I was going to continue to show up with as much energy, passion, and enthusiasm as I could. I wanted to be remembered as someone who did her job well. *Not irreplaceable, just hard to replace.*

I had another opportunity to practice this when I was working as a fitness instructor. Some days, I would show up to class and the room would be full; we ran out of equipment on more than one occasion. Other times, I would show up to teach and only one person would be there. They would always say, "I'm happy to just go on the treadmill if you don't want to teach just to me." I would respond with, "I'm not teaching today. We're working out together." I left the front of the room, turned around to face the mirror, and *taught* the class alongside the only participant.

We shouldn't base our enthusiasm, contribution, and engagement on the number of people that show up, or the commitment we have to a cause. We need to base our enthusiasm and engagement on the fact that we are someone who shows up as the best version of themselves!

8. Lead with Love

The entire chapter about leading from fear was essentially prompting the message of leading with love, but I feel it bears repeating. Love in this context is not the warm and fuzzy feeling we get with our closest friends. It's not the feelings of lust we get with a significant other. It's not the endless and unconditional love that we feel with our family. This type of love is about a set of responses and behaviors that we can use to build healthy relationships with people regardless of how we feel personally toward them.

This type of love is truly about being a kind human and creating a ripple effect of kindness. We can start a ripple effect of kindness when we enter into a conversation with someone using an optimistic attitude, that individual approaches their next interaction with a more positive approach, and so on. Leading with love means showing up with curiosity and a positive attitude. Every time we have an interaction with someone, we can either make their day better or worse. So let's make it better!

Leading with love means we give people the benefit of the doubt. When we are having a conversation, it's best to assume positive intent from the other person, especially if the interaction seems less than desirable (in our opinion). It is beneficial to both parties to assume the best—that the comment came from a positive place and not out of malice. This mantra has saved me so many times. It continuously helps me come back to being responsible *to* people and not *for* people. Repeating the phrase, *always assume positive intent,* helps me take things less personally, remaining able to lead with love and not overthink interactions with others.

9. Create Space

Like many leaders, parents, or any adult for that matter, I have a hard time sitting still. I have a hard time not feeling guilty if I am sitting and relaxing while there are things to be done … and there always are.

When I was pregnant with my daughter, I realized that lying in *savasana*, or corpse pose, (flat on the floor, arms by your sides) while practicing yoga, made me cry every time. It was the only time during the week that I had no distractions. There was no TV in the background, no audiobook or podcast playing, no music to pay attention to—it was just me and my thoughts. I was always very thankful for this emotional release. As someone who never sits still, it wasn't very often that I allowed myself to think my own thoughts.

Four years after I had my daughter, and two years after my mom passed away, I had a discovery call with a potential business coach. Within 20 minutes of meeting me, she called me out, "You need to turn off all of the noise for 30 days. Turn off the content, stop reading books, stop listening to music. You need to think your own thoughts." Tears immediately filled my eyes, and I felt scared. I didn't know how to turn off the constant intake of information. I didn't want to think about what it would look like to not be learning. Subconsciously, I'm guessing I didn't really want to hear what my mind had to say when I finally took the time to listen to it. I only made it through 15 days of her 30-day challenge to *turn off the noise*, but it sparked a level of self-awareness that I had been lacking before.

I know when I'm getting too busy. I can feel the overwhelm starting to seep in, and because of this, I have started to *embrace confident underwhelm*. I need to turn off the noise and feel good about turning my phone off. I want to take a walk without worrying that I wasn't adding steps to my watch. I want to be able to spend time with my kids without feeling guilty that I wasn't checking something off of my to-do list. I want to be confident when doing things that don't always move the needle forward. I want to be in control, both of my intentional movement forward and my ability to turn off the noise, create space for myself, sit in the silence with my own thoughts, and enjoy the moments as they come. I don't want to be overwhelmed, as in bored or uninspired; I want to be underwhelmed by outside noise and expectations, so can enjoy the moments of stillness when nothing is being completed and not feel overwhelmed by my lack of progress.

A few months after I hired this incredible woman to be my business coach, she offered a free breathwork session. Breathwork is a practice of intentionally breathing to release toxins and stress when you breathe out, and nourish your mind and body when you breathe in.[37] It was extremely far out of my comfort zone. Despite being uncomfortable, I wanted to experience this new thing everyone on my social media feed was claiming to be a game changer for their business. During the 30-minute breathwork session, my coach kept having us repeat, "I am worthy to take up space." (Breathwork produced the same type of emotion in me that lying in savasana did.) Immediately following the session, I knew I needed to dive deeper into this word, *space*. I even went as far as choosing it as my word of the year. It had so many meanings, and I knew as I continued to become more self-aware that it would be a great reminder to put an emphasis on growing myself and my influence with others.

Some of the different ways I have incorporated space into my world are:

- **Believing** that I am worthy to take up space. It's one thing to say it out loud and to show up in a way that portrays confidence to others. It's another thing entirely to *believe* that we are worthy to take up space, to speak up and have our voices heard. It takes a lot of repetition

---

37 https://www.webmd.com/balance/what-is-breathwork

and work to truly believe that we are worthy to be wherever we are and unapologetically claim that space for yourself. I am still working on this every day. (For additional help in believing you are worthy, look back on the second tier of the foundation of self.)

- **Creating** space for myself looks like going on walks with no other distractions. It looks like waking up earlier in the morning for the peace and quiet I crave.

I was having a conversation with someone around the word *space*, and that person immediately assumed that by *space* I was talking about solitude. The person questioned me about how they could have space with multiple kids, a spouse, a job, and other responsibilities. But space doesn't mean we're doing things alone. We can create space for others to join us. We can ask questions that encourage them to take the mic and speak their opinions. We can create an opportunity for them to join us as we work on ourselves, whether that's exercising together, starting a book club, going on walks with one another, or inviting another family to join us for supper. Creating space for others to shine will help us to elevate our influence and set an example of what it looks like for others to do the same.

- **Entering** spaces that we want to be a part of. For me, this looked like joining a gym, when I realized that I had more fun working out as part of a team. It involved going to networking events that I had convinced myself I didn't have time for, even though I was craving the community they provided. I found a community of women online who were working toward building their businesses. It helped so much to have the influence of others who were in the same season of life that I was in.

This is another reminder that in order to live the life that we want, it's important to remember that we get to *choose* that life. We have to put intentional action and effort toward creating and entering the spaces that we want to be a part of.

The biggest way I began creating more space for myself was the result of a study I read in Jess Ekstrom's book, *Chasing the Bright Side,* the same book I referred to earlier when talking about how our excuses are also choices. After rereading the passage in the book, I realized I hadn't followed the advice exactly. I had interpreted the message in a way that served me in that season. So, here's how I interpreted it: when we get distracted, it's our body's way of telling us something that our conscious mind is likely missing: *we need a break!*

Every time I read a book and find myself having to restart a paragraph, or sometimes a whole page, I know I need to take a break. Or when I am listening to an audiobook or podcast, and I have to keep rewinding it because I have been daydreaming and didn't comprehend anything from the past few minutes, I know I need to take a break.

I remind myself that I need to create space in that moment for my mind and body to decompress and come back to neutral. I take a walk, play with my kids, exercise, journal, or sometimes just watch TV, so I can tune out and laugh at something irrelevant to my day. This practice of catching myself every time I begin to get distracted has helped decrease the overwhelm of feeling like I always need to be learning, consuming, moving, and contributing. I have to take space sometimes to just relax and decompress.

10. Radical Responsibility

One of the presentations I typically give to high schoolers and college students is titled "Building Confidence from Scratch." The central message comes down to this:

> We are our own persons, and we are our own responsibility. Building confidence is a practice of trial and error, but ultimately, it's about consistency. It's a matter of evaluating our excuses so we realize that we can trust ourselves to do what we need to do. We can't hide behind a persona that we have to work to keep up. It's a process to figure out how to be our real selves and show up unapologetically in our relationships. But taking responsibility for our decisions means that we trust ourselves and that we aren't afraid to fail.

An important message to share with the younger generations is that as parents, teachers, and bosses, it's hard to know when to start holding our tongues. When should we start allowing them to either succeed or fail on their own? When is the right time to start letting them learn from their mistakes, especially when we know we could have saved them the time and discomfort?

The ability to build confidence is contingent on us taking responsibility for what we can control. As a child, student, and/or employee, the moment we take radical responsibility, our mindset will shift from, *Why aren't you doing this for me,* to *I trust myself to do this on my own.*

So, as a parent, teacher, or leader, what is our role in this? How can we make someone care about something? It's unfortunate, but there are people who do not care. A lot of the times, the indifference to learning and growing comes down to a few things:

1. They have a fear of the unknown.
2. They feel like they aren't trusted by others.
3. They've never been held accountable, so they don't know what it looks like.
4. They have a lack of confidence in their own skills, abilities, and follow-through.

A lot of these concerns can be debunked by someone in authority simply saying to them, *I trust you. I trust you to do what you need to do, using your unique strengths to do it your way. Here's the expectation (_____), here are the boundaries (_____), and I'm here to help if you need it, but I trust you.*

We need to express our trust in them while simultaneously offering our help, if needed.

No one can truly feel responsible for their actions if someone is always there to correct them or bail them out if things go awry. Whether we're sharing this message with someone we wish would step up to the plate, or we need to continue reminding ourselves that we are in control and worthy of trust (from yourself and those around you), our commitment and excitement about doing a good job changes.

As the child, student, or employee, if we feel like someone is always trying to correct us or fix things so we never fail, it is our responsibility to ask for the trust and opportunity to try things on our own, taking things into our own hands.

Take radical responsibility and discipline yourself so no one else has to!

So, where do we go from here? Several years ago during a workout class, we were near the end of the cooldown following an hour-long workout. The instructor summarized a study that said the cool-down is only as useful as the good feelings it gives us. It's not so much about the physical benefits of the cool-down, but the emotional feelings we get by having a few minutes to reflect on how hard we worked and how proud we should be of ourselves. It's a tool (or a trick) to get us coming back for more by covering up the fact that the process wasn't easy, but remembering that the results are worth it!

I never took time to validate the study, but here's how I look at it. You may not have agreed with everything I shared in this book, but like I say in the introduction to my podcast, "Take what you want, and leave what you don't."

As you finish this book, take a few moments to reflect on the amount of information you take in during a day. We all have so many voices speaking to us that we don't often stop and make space to think and listen to our own thoughts. You get to take what you want, and leave what you don't, in every context. Your voice is the most important one to listen to.

CONCLUSION

"Don't attach your worthiness to your results or ability. Attach your worth to your intentions."
- Desiree Petrich

One day, one hour, one moment can change our lives. The choices we make leading up to that turning point, and the decisions we make after, can be the difference between feeling like we are living a life we love and feeling like we're just trying to recover from one gut-punch after the other.

I'm obviously not flawless in this process of self-development. I wrote an entire chapter about the excuses I used to convince myself that I wasn't capable of overcoming the negative mindset that took 30 years to build. I also wrote an entire chapter outlining what it looks like to be taken down to rock bottom. But I am proud of the stories, the conversations, the mindset shifts, and the tough love I experienced during those times in my life. Sometimes, we just need a good kick in the butt to remind ourselves that we already have all of the tools and knowledge we need. We just have to choose to engage ourselves in the process and take intentional action.

Self-engagement is not all rainbows and sunshine, but as the first tier in the Foundation of Self framework, it's critical to start taking action. Learning to ask ourselves the right questions and answer them honestly takes a lot of courage and a whole lot of practice! To the outside world, self-engagement looks like implementing habits that reveal the changes we make and the actions we take. On the inside, it looks like a lot of internal dialogue. It's a much deeper process than what people can see.

I was presenting a lunch-and-learn workshop when someone raised their hand and said, "I talk to myself too often."

I responded with, "There is no such thing as talking to yourself too often. You are the person you spend the most time with. Your voice is the most important voice to listen to!"

I recently watched the Becoming Unstoppable event put on by Jamie Kern Lima. One of her guests, Matthew Hussy, said, "Familiarity breeds contempt." We are with ourselves 100 percent of the time. It's easy to fall in love with other people. They are exciting and surprising to us. On the other hand, we struggle to love ourselves because we are the only person we will spend every moment of our lives with. It makes sense that we begin to take ourselves for granted.

We have to reverse engineer the way we look at habits. We don't have to work out so we look better for others. We can move our bodies because they are the only ones we have, and we love ourselves so much that there is no question about *if*, but *when*. We get to set boundaries because we know that we are worthy of putting ourselves, our needs, and our families before anyone else's opinions or expectations. At work, we can continue to read, develop, learn, and grow, not to fill a job description, but because we love ourselves and know that we are worthy of dedicating the time to ourselves.

When we find ourselves being propelled, or dragged along, by anything other than our own intention, remember that walking into the wind (although uncomfortable) is the absolute best place to be when we are looking to grow. We get to decide where we want to go, set our direction, put our head down, and place one foot in front of the other. It's what we've been working for! The ability to put our needs first, while also being aware of the thoughts and point of view of those around us, can be our biggest asset. But we have to take the time to build our Foundation of Self, so we can foster our self-awareness in every area.

My hope for you after reading this book is to understand that you can simultaneously treat yourself *and* others with unconditional love. Remember, love is not about the feelings you have toward someone in any given moment; rather, it's a way of being. It's treating people with respect and understanding that everyone has their own set of circumstances behind why they do the things they do, even when we don't get to see the process behind their decisions.

I encourage you to individualize yourself. Write down what you like, and what you don't like. Create your own versions of success and work toward reaching them and celebrating them!

Understand your behavioral tendencies. Get to know yourself better by asking yourself questions. Begin to learn how your tendencies and personality traits coincide with others.

My hope for you is that you will take intentional action toward increasing your self-awareness. Learn to trust yourself to do the things that you say you're going to do. Learn to push through hard moments with both high expectations and grace. One of my favorite authors, Gretchen Rubin, says, *You can accept yourself, and still expect more from yourself.*[38]

I encourage you to cultivate relationships with those around you and show up unapologetically as your true self. Learn to lead with confidence. Understand that, in every situation, you have all of

---

[38]https://gretchenrubin.com/articles/secret-of-adulthood-accept-yourself-and-expect-more-from-yourself/

the tools and knowledge you need. You can't always control the thoughts that come into your head, but you can control the next thought and the actions that follow.

Learning to control at least some of our thoughts increases happiness. And, remember, happiness is a state of being. You don't have to *earn* it, and you don't ever have to *lose* it. Happiness can be the thing that you continue to come back to, even in moments of anger, frustration, guilt, and sadness. As long as you are in control of your self-engagement, your self-worth, and your self-awareness, you have everything you need to not only continue building a life you love but to thrive. *Be yourself;* it's everything you need to succeed!

RESOURCES

For all of the resources listed in the book: desireepetrich.com/book

To see some of my favorite products: desireepetrich.com/favorites

To view and print the Foundation of Self Framework graphics: desireepetrich.com/foundation

To download journaling exercises for the Foundation of Self Framework and register to attend the next live Foundation of Self workshop: desireepetrich.com/framework

To take your own (paid) DISC personality assessment: desireepetrich.com/disc

About the Author

Desiree Petrich is an author, speaker, corporate coach and trainer, and the host of the Lead With Confidence Podcast, as well as a Certified Practitioner of The Five Behaviors. She founded her company Intentional Action in 2022 after losing her mom unexpectedly just two months after bringing her son home from the NICU.

Desiree began her leadership journey as the manager of a dementia facility. After leading the company through the pandemic, she shifted out of healthcare and became the events coordinator for the local chamber of commerce. This experience caused her to fall in love with all things business, community, teamwork, networking, and growth.

Desiree's focus is helping high achievers become great leaders. Through intentional leadership and high-performance coaching, workshop development, keynote speaking and unique teambuilding activities, she has been able to share her love of personal and professional development with others.

To make development opportunities more accessible, Desiree has started hosting leadership conferences, with the first one, the Intentional Leadership Summit, held on August 7, 2024, at Grace Life Church in Marshall, Minn.

Desiree's podcast Lead With Confidence focuses on helping individuals to know themselves better so they can show up in their own life with confidence and belief in themselves to choose the life they want to lead.

Desiree is a mom of two, avid reader, exercise lover, John Maxwell-certified team member, DISC consultant, and an advocate that everyone is entitled to a fulfilled life of their choosing.

Connect with Desiree

Website

desireepetrich.com

Social Links

https://www.linkedin.com/in/desiree-petrich/

https://www.instagram.com/desireepetrich/

https://www.facebook.com/profile.php?id=100090653712433

LEAD WITH CONFIDENCE
PODCAST

WITH DESIREE PETRICH

Head over to desireepetrich.com/podcast, or search *lead with confidence* anywhere you get your podcasts to join me every week to learn what it means to lead with confidence. It's the best place to become intentional about *choosing the life you lead*.

Leading with confidence looks like belief. It manifests as a belief in yourself that, no matter the situation you find yourself in, you have the tools, the mindset, and the knowledge to overcome any obstacle.

My goal is to uncover the stories and lessons of those who lead by example, to learn what their formula is for success, because guess what... The formula is different for everyone! So take what you want, and leave what you don't. We are here to learn and grow together!

Apple Podcasts Link

https://podcasts.apple.com/us/podcast/lead-with-confidence/id1715587637

Spotify Podcasts Link

https://open.spotify.com/show/3X0yI29A8h3iqJju9kW4Ge

INTENTIONAL ACTION WITH DESIREE PETRICH

Resources

At desireepetrich.com, you will find all the resources you need to grow yourself and your team into intentional leaders with a commitment to being the best that you can be.

To learn more about coaching, workshops, keynotes, and how we can work together, book a call. **desireepetrich.com/contact**

Programs such as:

Climb to Confident Leadership – Emerging Leader Program
Intentional Leader Mastermind – thought leadership and networking
The Leadership Game – teambuilding activity
The Five Dysfunctions of a Team – workshops, lunch & learns, etc.
The Five Behaviors – workshops, lunch & learns, etc.
Lead With Confidence and 5 Rules for Life – keynotes and breakout sessions.
Foundation of Self – goal setting workshop
DISC – workshops and team assessments.

Visit desireepetrich.com to learn more.

Intentional Leader Summit
Elevate Your Influence

The Intentional Leader Summit focuses on the growth of the individual. From the maintenance team to the C-suite, and from customer service to the engineering team, this summit provides a message directed at the responsibility of every employee to be their best self. To lead by example at work, at home, and in their community. To live a life they love at home and at work.

Incredible keynote speakers and breakout sessions will have participants leaving feeling inspired and empowered to elevate their influence in all walks of life.

Visit desireepetrich.com/summit to learn more about this in-person leadership conference in Marshall, Minn.

HELP PLEASE!

More than anything I hope you were able to find yourself in the pages of this book, and that you feel inspired to begin building a life that you love!

I appreciate that you took the time to go on this journey with me, and I would love to hear your feedback and takeaways.

If you loved this book, it would mean the world to me if you could take two minutes to leave a helpful review on Amazon letting me know what you thought of the book:

Desireepetrich.com/review

Thank you so much!

Desiree Petrich

www.ingramcontent.com/pod-product-compliance
Lightning Source LLC
Chambersburg PA
CBHW051001140626
46546CB00017B/2126